Simon & Schuster Canada
A Division of Simon & Schuster, Inc.
166 King Street East, Suite 300
Toronto, Ontario M5A 1J3

This Simon & Schuster Canada edition April 2020

SIMON & SCHUSTER CANADA and colophon are trademarks of Simon & Schuster, Inc.

For information about special discounts for bulk purchases, please contact Simon & Schuster Special Sales at 1-800-268-3216 or CustomerService@simonandschuster.ca.

Manufactured in the United States of America

10 9 8 7 6 5 4 3 2 1

Library and Archives Canada Cataloguing in Publication

Title: City and Country / Sarah Richardson.
Names: Richardson, Sarah, 1971- author.
Description: Series statement: Collected ; 1
Identifiers: Canadiana (print) 20190165871
Canadiana (ebook) 2019016588X
ISBN 9781982140366 (softcover)
ISBN 9781982140380 (ebook)
Subjects: LCSH: Interior decoration.
Classification: LCC NK2115 .R52 2020 | DDC 747—dc23

ISBN 978-1982-14036-6
ISBN 978-1982-14038-0 (ebook)

Editorial Director Beth Hitchcock
Art Director Rose Pereira

Cover Photography Valerie Wilcox

Collected

BY SARAH RICHARDSON

VOLUME N° 1

City + Country

PUBLISHED BY SIMON & SCHUSTER
NEW YORK · LONDON · TORONTO · SYDNEY · NEW DELHI

PHOTOGRAPHY BY STACEY BRANDFORD

Contents

Welcome to *Collected*, the first in a new series of books that answer the question "Sarah, what are you loving right now?" It's not a simple answer. I believe that "opposites attract" applies to design just as much as what I love. I live in the city but consider myself more than a little bit country. Would I rather buy a linear mid-century modern table or a rough-hewn piece with peeling paint? Both, of course! That's why, for the debut issue, we're exploring fresh-air spaces that make you think of warm summer breezes and the sweet smell of hay right alongside cool abodes tucked into buzzing urban neighbourhoods. Each theme will play with opposites—will the next one be Colour + Neutrals or Past + Present? Stay tuned for Volume 2, coming to a bookseller near you this fall!

CITY OR COUNTRY STYLE: WHICH ONE ARE YOU?

Our first edition of *Collected* is all about contrast, so we asked the people behind the pages to tell us where their soul lives.

EDITORIAL TEAM

Oh, I'm country, without a doubt. Give me wide-open windows, rustic wood, vintage ironstone platters, and bed linens dried on the line any day.

BETH HITCHCOCK
Editorial Director

When I travel, I'm drawn to the energy of cities like Los Angeles, New York, and Lisbon. But my real fantasy is to live in a Frank Lloyd Wright–inspired home set in rolling hills.

ROSE PEREIRA
Art Director

SRD TEAM

They say you can't take the country out of the girl, and quaintness has become a part of my design DNA. I'll always choose warm, textural elements with a well-loved patina as the foundation for my eclectic style.

JENNIFER GIBEAU
Media Manager,
Sarah Richardson Design

Despite my rural and coastal origins, the cities of Scandinavia have left their mark on my design aesthetic the most. I'm all for minimalism, pale woods, and neutral tones for a hygge home.

COLLEEN MAHAFFIE
Marketing Coordinator,
Sarah Richardson Design

That's like asking me to pick my favourite child! I love them equally. In the city, you really have to think about longevity and how people live the majority of their lives. In the country, you get to take chances and do things you might not normally do.

NATALIE HODGINS
Designer, "Heritage Classic"

I'm lucky enough to enjoy the best of both worlds: After nearly two decades of city living, I moved back to the country (and bought a cottage, too). I love the buzz of my work life in the city, then I get to retreat to the country at the end of the day.

LINDSAY MENS CRAIG
Designer, "Urban Cottage" and "Coastal Colonial"

I like a little country with my city and a little city with my country. Too much of a good thing is not a good thing, so the country spaces I design include an elegant moment; the same goes for country elements in what might become a stuffy city environment.

TOMMY SMYTHE
Designer, "Coastal Colonial"

I'm both a city and beach person, because I grew up next to the ocean. I spend about 80% of my time in the city and 20% of my time by the beach.

SUSANA SIMONPIETRI
Designer, "Style Factory"

Everything that speaks to retreat is closer to our hearts. We find true joy in creating homes for our clients that have that special soul, that place for gathering and getting away.

RICHARD OUELETTE & MAXIME VANDAL
Designers, "French Accent"

I love creating spaces where people can connect with nature. Inspired by the raw beauty of the Pacific Northwest, I use natural materials suited to a country environment.

SOPHIE BURKE,
Designer, "Mid-Century Marvel"

I have an eclectic style, so I like to incorporate a little country into my city home—softening up modern lines makes it feel cozy.

VALERIE WILCOX
Photographer

City style is the closest to me. Maybe it's because I like the challenge of making my interior space an oasis when living in an otherwise concrete environment.

STACEY BRANDFORD
Photographer

I grew up in the city (and am still here), so my mind loves the city but my heart loves the country more and more. I guess that means I'm a country girl?

VIRGINIA MACDONALD
Photographer

"THIS IS ONE OF THE OLDEST HOUSES IN THE NEIGHBOURHOOD, SO WE WANTED TO MAINTAIN THE CHARACTER, CELEBRATE THE DETAIL, AND INFUSE EACH ROOM WITH A LIGHTER, MORE STREAMLINED DIRECTION."

The breakfast room captures the spirit of the whole house: a traditional envelope layered with vintage and contemporary elements. A Persian rug delivers pattern and colour while dark floors and charcoal grey–painted window sashes give the space modern flair.

Heritage Classic

DESIGN BY NATALIE HODGINS & SARAH RICHARDSON
PHOTOGRAPHY BY STACEY BRANDFORD

5

DESIGN BY
**NATALIE HODGINS
& SARAH RICHARDSON,**
SARAH RICHARDSON DESIGN

TORONTO, ONTARIO

3,700 SQUARE FEET

128 YEARS OLD

4 BEDROOMS

3.5 BATHROOMS

3-YEAR RENOVATION

1 DOG SHOWER

←

MAKE AN ENTRANCE

A tomato-red door and black-green outside trim make a handsome combination against red brick. The black paint echoes the charcoal blue used in the inside.

→

What a difference a window makes! In the entryway, a new porthole window flanked by LED sconces injects a contemporary note and brightens up what was once a dark passageway. Dark trim acts as a cooling agent to the warmth of terra-cotta tiles.

THIS GRAND REDBRICK Victorian is a study in the two Rs: renovation and reincarnation. While the home boasted some glorious architectural details, like original fireplaces and staircases, it had gone through less-than-glorious renovations in the 1970s and '80s. By the time the current homeowners, an empty-nest couple, purchased the home, it was important to get the feeling just right. "It's not any one look," says designer Natalie Hodgins. "It's curated just for them. Every single item is here because they loved it and we loved it, and it all came together beautifully." Sarah says the result brings a spirit of renewal to the home. "Many of the pieces have lived a past life, so it's all about celebrating what you've got and reinterpreting it for a new beginning."

← A grasscloth-covered sideboard anchors the wall beneath one of the homeowner's photos, taken in Antarctica. Looking to create just the right vignette? Mix three objects of varying heights and widths that echo the palette of the room.

YES, YOU CAN!
Add a marble top to a sideboard so it acts as a durable surface for entertaining (especially when that marble is a leftover piece from the fireplace surround).

"When you combine antique art, vintage furniture, and bold contemporary fabric, the result is a mix that feels new and now."

—Sarah Richardson

↑
The original living room mantel was restored, while the hearth and surround were replaced with honed marble. A mid-century-style chair with cord-wrapped arms provides lightness in the inky-hued room and is a deceptively comfortable spot for fireside reading.

YES, YOU CAN!

Install a gallery wall yourself—test the pattern on the floor before hanging.

←

Pick a line, any line! To create cohesion with a variety of frame sizes, think about horizontal alignment. Here, the top two rows are aligned by the bottom of the frames and the bottom row is aligned by the top of the frames.

Wall Colour:
Matchstick (2013) by Farrow & Ball

↑
To make the large dining room feel bold but bright, the end walls were papered in patterned inky-blue grass cloth while the side walls were painted rich cream.

"If you're renovating and have important treasures or sentimental pieces that you want to blend in, plan ahead and let them lead the design rather than make them fit as an afterthought." —SR

"The home grew out of a diverse collection of art, vintage rugs, and some iconic furniture pieces that, when blended, proves you can mix styles and create a space that is cohesive. The trick is only introducing items that you love."

—Natalie Hodgins

↑
1 SOFA, 2 LOOKS

The same sofa gets two different style statements on opposite sides of the living room: One's topped with contemporary art, and the other is nestled into a bay window dressed with roman shades in a painterly brushstroke print. The sofas, designed by Sarah, are upholstered in creamy oatmeal chenille and sit on a plinth for a mid-century modern profile—"No vacuuming underneath required!" adds Sarah.

YES, YOU CAN!

Build the palette for an entire room from
the ground up. Start with a great rug and
extract all the colours for an amazing result.

"The kitchen mandate was a chic space with hearty materials and style for miles. The black slate floor was the winner in a room that welcomes four grandchildren, large dogs, and lots of foot traffic when entertaining." —NH

DETAILS WE LOVE

1- Tip-cut slate tiles laid in a chevron pattern put a twist on tradition.

2- A bank of L-shaped cabinetry maxes storage, function, and visual impact on a tricky angled wall.

3- The warm-and-cool mix of brass and steel proves you don't have to choose!

4- Brass banding turns the range hood into the sparkling jewel of the kitchen.

↑
The long, narrow space provided some challenges, but ultimately accommodated an eight-foot island, a bar, a pantry, a desk, a breakfast nook, and French doors to the yard.

Cabinet Colour:
Wolf Gray (2127-40)
by Benjamin Moore

Beadboard Backing Colour:
Wickham Gray (HC-171)
by Benjamin Moore

↓
Solid walnut shelves wrapped in brass brackets provide some breathing room in a richly hued kitchen with plenty of closed storage.

COMING CLEAN

An indulgence? Perhaps. But, if you've got a ravine-adjacent home and a pooch who loves to explore, carving out space in the basement for a dog shower might seem more like a necessity than a luxury.

Renovating allows you to reinterpret a home for how you live. This unfinished basement became the "laundry lab" for its combination of amazing storage and functional work space.

YES, YOU CAN!
Mix navy cabinets with a charcoal sink and black slate floors for some dark drama.

↑
Tongue-and-groove panelling on the ceiling, a rug, and even a chandelier give the laundry room a decorated feeling that goes with the rest of the house. "If you have the time, space, and budget, why not make every room awesome?" says Sarah.

Upper Cabinet Colour: Wickham Gray (HC-171) by Benjamin Moore
+
Lower Cabinet Colour: Hale Navy (HC-154) by Benjamin Moore

DETAILS WE LOVE

1- If one bubble lamp makes a statement, a group of five is downright dynamite.

2- A long, low fireplace wall with white brick reinforces the horizontal orientation of the architecture.

3- Squeeze in more seating with a built-in floating hearth bench.

4- Tall, black-framed windows call attention to the ceiling height.

5- In a bright white space, wraparound walnut shelves add warmth, comfort, and storage.

1

2

"MY GOAL FOR THIS HOME'S INTERIOR? TO BALANCE A STREAMLINED MODERN AESTHETIC WITH THE WEST COAST LIFESTYLE OF A YOUNG FAMILY."
—

Mid-Century Marvel

DESIGN BY **SOPHIE BURKE**

PHOTOGRAPHY BY **EMA PETER**

DESIGN BY
SOPHIE BURKE,
SOPHIE BURKE
DESIGN

NORTH
VANCOUVER,
BRITISH
COLUMBIA

3,901 SQUARE
FEET

1-YEAR BUILD

4 BEDROOMS

4 BATHROOMS

2 PARENTS,
2 KIDS

1 DOG, 1 CAT

1 PINK DOOR

YES, YOU CAN!
Why default to drywall when
you can make a partition wall a
design feature with custom
back-to-back shelves? Genius!

↑
NATURAL WONDERS

The home backs onto a greenbelt, so noncombustible materials had to be used for a certain percentage of the exterior. Black metal does the trick while making a bold modern statement.

←

A pink door echoes the Louis Poulsen pendant light—a mid-century modern icon—and softens up the home's black exterior.

Door Colour:
Calamine (230) by Farrow & Ball

"**B**RIGHT, OPEN, AIRY, clean-lined"—those are just a few of the words designer Sophie Burke uses to describe her clients' North Vancouver house. The four-bedroom home was a new-build, which gave Sophie a blank canvas to showcase the kind of horizontal lines, iconic light fixtures, and occasional bursts of colour that would look right at home in a mid-century mecca like Palm Springs. But even more important than the home's fixtures and furnishings was a connection to the outdoors. "The house backs onto a greenbelt, so sight lines and easy access to the back and side yards was a must," she says. With an abundance of windows and fully retractable sliding doors, the result is a four-seasons playground for the couple's two young kids and two pets.

↓
Colour-blocked art made by the sister of one of the homeowners acts as the sole injection of colour. Art-installation tip: Match the horizontal and vertical spacing to make a group of ten read as one.

White oak stairs
and a minimal white
handrail and spindles
make the modern
staircase appear
to float.

"White oak flooring gives the
whole house a fresh feeling while
being durable for a family.
The millwork accents are
walnut to give us that nod to
mid-century style and tie in with
existing furniture pieces."

—Sophie Burke

SERENITY NOW

←

A touch of pink—the female homeowner's favourite—gives just a whisper of pretty to the minimal principal bedroom. Wraparound corner windows without trim create a contemporary light box.

↓

Organic shapes, white features (like the standout soaker tub), and black outlines don't compete with the lush view—the bathroom is like a spa in the woods.

"The powder room is an ideal space to express personality. Green is an integral colour to the home with the surrounding forest framed by all the windows." —SB

YES, YOU CAN!
Create a continuous wrap of tile by carrying a single hit of fabulous from floor to wall and capping it with a floating shelf.

↓
Even the windows get in on the mid-century riff and are placed intentionally to maximize views of the greenbelt. Two sliding door systems connect the dining room and living room to the patio, which extends the living space year-round.

YES, YOU CAN!

Work with what you have: Two family heirloom dressers anchor the wall of windows.

← Flat-front cabinets with no hardware make the kitchen disappear into the walls and keep the focus on the windows and views.

↓ Heaters make the outdoor covered living room a great space to gather, even on chilly days.

"The indoor-outdoor connection of the dining room with the covered outdoor living area is the epitome of west-coast living. It's such a fantastic feature for this family to enjoy!" –SB

↑
Keep the history but make it your own—an original dark coffered ceiling gave the living room historic character but felt too heavy. Painting the beams white and adding beadboard panels makes everything old feel fresh and new.

"I WANTED TO GIVE MY FAMILY A HOME THAT'S COZY WITH LOTS OF LAYERS AND TEXTURES. IT MAY LOOK ELEGANT, BUT THERE'S NOTHING TOO PRECIOUS HERE."

YES, YOU CAN!

Vintage lamps get an update thanks to custom shades with painted and gilded bands that take the bases from simple to sensational.

Urban Cottage

DESIGN BY LINDSAY MENS CRAIG

PHOTOGRAPHY BY STACEY BRANDFORD

DESIGN BY
**LINDSAY
MENS CRAIG,**
SARAH
RICHARDSON
DESIGN

TORONTO,
ONTARIO

2,500 SQUARE
FEET

100 YEARS OLD

50 YEARS SINCE
THE LAST RENO

4 BEDROOMS

2 BATHROOMS

1 DIY HUSBAND

2 DAUGHTERS

1 DOG

FAVOURITE THINGS

→

Faced with a dated vision of green and brown, Lindsay (with Kennedy, 6) wanted to keep her home's charm but give the exterior an overhaul on a tight budget. Some warm white paint brightened up the porch and gave the Craftsman-style home a boost of curb appeal.

↓

Lindsay is known for her love of colour and pattern, but when it comes to her own home, you'll find her embracing a decidedly coastal palette: "I've experimented and lived with other colours, but they just don't make me as happy as blue."

YOU COULD SAY designer Lindsay Mens Craig is an old soul. Rather than tear down the faded, 100-year-old home in Toronto's west end, she chose to fix it up. Her challenge? To give the charming Craftsman-style house a youthful spin for herself, husband Mike, and their two daughters. Lindsay worked with what she couldn't change (like a bossy coffered ceiling in the living room), and transformed what she could (like opening up the main floor). "We put in a lot of elbow grease and called in some favours from my carpenter brother," she says with a laugh. The result is a clean, cheerful backdrop for Lindsay's collection of vintage pieces, and a testament to the power of seeing potential.

YES, YOU CAN!

Go for "falsies" when privacy isn't an issue. Instead of investing in custom romans (and all that extra fabric), a deep valance adds softness.

SMART SOLUTIONS

←

When looking for
the ultimate pattern
mix, you'll never
go wrong with
a balanced ratio
of stripes, florals,
geometrics, and
mini-prints.

↑

Craving bistro
style with a dash
of practicality?
A marble subway-tile
backsplash delivers
natural beauty while
quartz counters
offer the durability
that family life
demands.

→

When the right
fixture doesn't
exist, find a custom
solution! A salvaged
vintage shade and
parts were paired
with a new backplate
and post to create
a sconce to match
the vintage pendants
above the peninsula.

If you've participated in a "his 'n' hers" renovation project, you'll know that blending styles can be an exercise in compromise. When Mike selected a painting with rich, earthy hues, Lindsay reinforced its palette by adding a cognac leather ottoman to the mix. The result is a cozy den that marries masculine and feminine elements.

↓

DETAILS WE LOVE

1- The fireplace, once an eyesore, got a Cinderella makeover with limestone veneer. A simple painted poplar mantel and bookshelves turn the wall into a feature that includes storage.

2- A bargain-basement vintage chandelier was reborn with a few replacement strands of crystals.

3- Mantel symmetry with an artistic twist: Tucking a couple pieces of freestanding art into a mirrored setting loosens up the formality and provides the freedom to swap them out whenever you like.

"I'm very nostalgic. My grandmother loved blue and birds. Believe it or not, Kennedy picked out this paper from all the options I brought her when she was just 3 years old."

—Lindsay Mens Craig

←
A hint of blue paint adds impact to the existing built-in storage drawers tucked into the roof.

Chair Colour:
Secret Garden (1284)
by Benjamin Moore
+
Ceiling Colour:
Silver Marlin
(2139-50) by
Benjamin Moore

YES, YOU CAN!
Old gilded frames become an evolving display for art and crafts when filled with a bulletin board from the dollar store.

→

COLOUR THEORY

When decorating for wee ones, practicality matters. Installing an inexpensive chair rail allowed Lindsay to paint the lower portion of the walls in a scrubbable paint finish and treat the upper portion to a gilded star–patterned wallpaper that wraps up and over the sloped ceilings.

Half-Wall Colour:
Mauve Blush
(2115-40) by
Benjamin Moore

A gallery wall doesn't need to fit into a perfect grid. Matching white mats act as the linking element in a grouping filled with sentimental treasures—needlepoint, a collection of family keys, gifts from friends and colleagues, and the first piece of art Lindsay ever bought all live cohesively together.

↓
Stuck with a narrow space? Lindsay designed the vanity at 7 feet long and only 19 inches deep (instead of the standard 22), which was made possible by wall-mounted faucets.

"This is the only bathroom upstairs, so I was determined to fit in two sinks no matter how narrow the room was!" —LMC

"WE WERE LUCKY TO INHERIT THE BEAMS AND BRICK
AND THAT'S WHAT MADE THE PROJECT SO EXCITING.
OUR JOB WAS TO MAKE THE SPACE INTIMATE, COZY,
COMFORTABLE, AND KID-FRIENDLY."

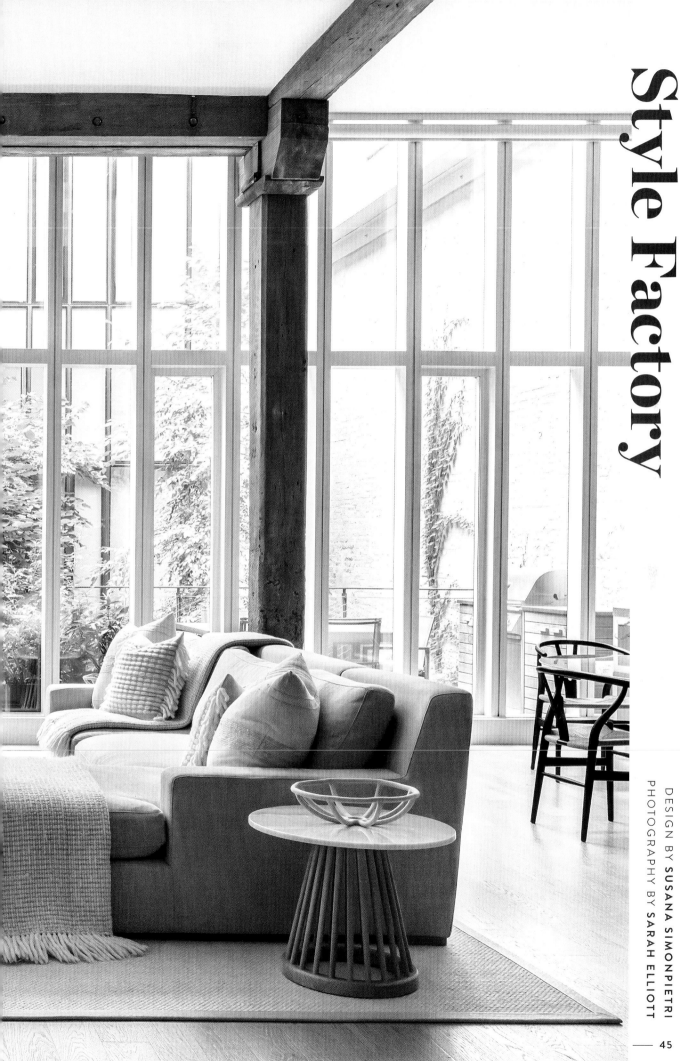

Style Factory

DESIGN BY SUSANA SIMONPIETRI

PHOTOGRAPHY BY SARAH ELLIOT

DESIGN BY
**SUSANA
SIMONPIETRI,**
CHANGO & CO.

BROOKLYN,
NEW YORK

3,700 SQUARE
FEET

4 BEDROOMS

3.5 BATHROOMS

2 PARENTS,
2 KIDS

2 CEILING
SWINGS

6-MONTH
RENOVATION

↓
FUN FEATURES
Think big when dealing with tall ceilings.
A single piece of art—a celestial tapestry
by Swedish textile designer Barbro Nilsson—
balances all the red brick and references the
city night skies outside the 13-foot windows.

→
Loft living is about making your own rules and
living the way you want to. If a formal dining
room isn't your thing, turn it into something
else—in this case, an open playroom for two
young kids, complete with swings.

YES, YOU CAN!
Expand your
definition of wall
art. Mounting a
textile inside a
shadow box creates
a one-of-a-kind
statement with rich
texture.

A FORMER BRILLO PAD factory in Dumbo, Brooklyn, is an exercise in pushing the envelope. That's because the bare-bones space was awe-inspiring but not quite to the homeowners' liking. Enter design firm Chango & Co.: "The clients were fans of our work, and they wanted this brick and beam space to feel like our past projects," says designer Susana Simonpietri. "Just an overall fun and easygoing style—kid-friendly, comfortable, accident-forgiving, and oversized." Out came the all-white kitchen for cerused oak cabinets with more warmth, and open living spaces were split into smaller zones for lounging, eating, and playing. But the biggest challenge was also the loft's biggest asset—its 13-foot ceilings. Where the clients had struggled to fill the vertical space, the designers worked to bring it down to eye level with artwork, statement ceiling pendants, and even two swings. Now, the hard loft shows its softer side for the whole family.

↓
Rift-cut cerused oak cabinets are framed within an oak panel painted white to blend in with the wall. This subtle move creates definition in a kitchen without walls.

"The kitchen is the first thing you see when you walk in the space. White oak cabinets have just the right amount of warmth and texture for a cozy family home." —Susana Simonpietri

DETAILS WE LOVE

1- An inset cooking and cleanup zone wrapped in white Caesarstone is set within the back wall and surrounded by sleek storage.

2- A single display shelf injects some softness into the millwork with the ability to showcase practical and pretty things.

3- Fully panelled and "barely there" appliances make this kitchen feel more furnished than functional.

4- An inset cooktop is streamlined and modern, while the oven is cleverly hidden in the island, so both are rarely seen from the living spaces.

↓
When it comes to vignette styling, less is more. A pair of airy glass lamps anchor the ends of an extra-long console table, as chunky baskets blend in with all the wood and provide a sneaky spot for storage.

What's the secret to a unified gallery wall when using three different frame finishes? Adhering to a strict palette of cream, black, and white allows the eye to focus on the harmony of the overall grouping.

YES, YOU CAN!
Hang multiple gallery groupings on one long wall— but make sure there's a visual break, like a doorway, mirror, or armoire.

"The clients had a collection of Damien Hirst butterflies, so we kept the room very neutral knowing how bright the art would be." –ss

In the boy's room, a fun playhouse-style bed minimizes the voluminous ceiling and makes one of the loft's littlest residents feel right at home. A neutral palette allows the bright toys to do the talking: "We find that's the best way for children to take ownership of their rooms," says Susana.

The four posters on a tester bed create an intimate space within the master bedroom, and the organic shape of the ceiling fixture relates back to the bed's greyed wood frame.

The baby girl's
nursery was
designed with
storage in mind but
also a sense of fun,
thanks to splashes
of neon pink and
items that beg
to be touched.

YES, YOU CAN!

Layer a plush, small-
scale decorative rug
over a low-pile
area rug.

"When you look at the kids' bath, all you see is bright blue dots, whimsical art, and tassle fringe, but none of that is permanent. We knew we could have fun with wallpaper since it's something that can be easily changed." –ss

IL FIORISTA
RESTAURANT

LITTLE BEACH
HOUSE HOTEL

LINNAEAN
SALON AND CAFÉ

INSPIRED
HEADBOARDS

SÃO LOURENÇO DO
BARROCAL RESORT

Global Edit

Our roundup of the most swoon-worthy city and country style from around the world.

EAT HERE

FLOWER POWER

It's a restaurant, it's a floral boutique, it's a learning centre! But let's face it: The real reason we're booking a table at Il Fiorista is because the design's as fresh as the food. Located in NoMad, just a petal's throw from New York's Flower District, the space has a powerful design pedigree: interiors by Elizabeth Roberts, furniture by Patricia Urquiola, and hand-painted murals by Leanne Shapton.
—

ilfioristanyc.com

**Love the Palette?
Get the Look:**

Serengeti Plain
90YY (48/255)
by Dulux

Spectra Blue
(2049-50) by
Benjamin Moore

Summer Melon
(2168-50) by
Benjamin Moore

Adobe Orange
(2171-30) by
Benjamin Moore

Babouche
(223) by
Farrow & Ball

Capitol Blue
30BB (18/190)
by Dulux

Blonde wood, pared-down twine details, and nubbly, neutral upholstery delivers Scandi-chic.

Who wouldn't want to order floral-infused cocktails at a bar like this? We'll take one of everything, please.

Simple checkerboard floors allow the groovy neo-'70s mural to bask in the spotlight. À la carte flowers are available to bring home.

BEACH CHIC

WHAT
Little Beach House

WHERE
Barcelona, Spain

WHY
Once a faded '50s hotel, the new hotspot got a "ready to mingle" look from the Soho House Group.
—
littlebeachhousebarcelona.com

DETAILS WE LOVE

1- Woven details wow with oceanside charm, from the humble ceiling fixtures to the rush backs and seats on the chairs.

2- Why be blah when a gallery could burst with colour? Three black picture lights punctuate the collection and emphasize the wall-to-wall install.

3- Lounge-ready pillows in a row, and all drawn from the painterly palette of the art.

4- Rounded tub chairs offer a cozy spot to tuck in for a drink.

COLLECTED CRUSH

IF YOU NEED US, WE'LL BE HERE

It's hard to imagine a more ooh-and-ahh-worthy destination for a massage or facial than Linnaean, a new wellness salon and café in London. If you can't make an overseas appointment, get inspired remotely. Martin Brudnizki Design Studio may have created the most blissful spa treatment room ever. We're loving the "everywhere" approach to the Christopher Farr Cloth Carnival wallpaper, not to mention the glorious green doors, trim, and floors.
—
linnaean.co.uk

WONDERWALL

Ever wondered how to give the wall behind your bed
a wake-up call? Two designers show you how.

Wall Colour:
Hague Blue (30)
by Farrow & Ball

PAPER IT

Nam Dang-Mitchell brings the outdoors
in with the tropical Jungle Land mural
from Rebel Walls. A cream and charcoal
palette gives it the sophisticated feel
of a vintage photo, while the furnishings and
décor deliver a thoroughly modern look.

TRIM IT

Looking to add architectural interest to a basic
wall? A simple panel moulding applied in a grid
pattern and painted deep blue creates a richly
detailed backdrop in a moody principal suite by
Feasby & Bleeks Design.

SEEING DOUBLE

Beloved for its sophisticated abstract quality, the Graffito print by Kelly Wearstler is popping up everywhere—and we're not mad about it. Paddington, Australia–based designer Tamsin Johnson puts the popular pattern to great use in two different, equally gorgeous ways.

WALLPAPER IN THE POWDER

Why be basic in a tiny jewel box of a room? The burnt terra-cotta colour of the wallpaper creates a dramatic context for a floating black marble sink.

FABRIC IN THE BEDROOM

Juxtaposed with the super-trad Noah's ark–themed Zambezi wallpaper from Cole & Son, Graffito shakes things up in the ultimate sweet-meets-stunning combo.

Gaga for Graffito? Check out more juicy colours, available through Kravet.

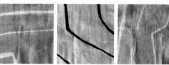

| Salmon Cream | Linen Onyx | Beige Ivory | Onyx Beige | Teal Pearl |

PHOTOGRAPHY BY MARK BURSTYN (BLUE WALL), NAM DANG-MITCHELL (MURAL), ANSON SMART (GRAPHIC WALLPAPER).

FARM FRESH

Looking to hit "pause" and slow down for a few days? The Portugal countryside is a design destination worth dreaming about.
—
barrocal.pt

Arches are a hot design motif, and their graceful curves soar up all over the resort. Here, chalky white walls, clay tile floors, and deep navy and teal accents draw you through the lobby bar's arched corridor.

Painted doors reflect the palette of the surrounding landscape.

Do picnics taste better when they emerge from a woven hamper under the shade of an olive tree? We're willing to find out.

Dress up a simple dining room with tapestries over dowels hung from the walls. It's a quick and low-commitment way to add wow factor.

IF YOU'RE LOOKING for magic, set your GPS to São Lourenço do Barrocal in Portugal's Alentejo region. This ancient farm village once housed fifty families—now, it's been reimagined as an understated luxury hotel. Simplicity reigns here, from the white-walled rooms where every adornment has a purpose, to the farm breakfasts and dinners that highlight the property's own organic vegetables. Stroll the vast property to exhale deeply and experience history: Even the pool is designed around one of sixteen dolmens (think: Stonehenge-style rocks) from the Neolithic Age. If activity's on the agenda, you can borrow bicycles, take a scenic horseback ride, float away in a hot-air balloon, or spend an afternoon at the spa (that counts as an activity, right?). As dusk settles and the sky turns cotton-candy pink, wander back along what was once the main street between buildings to relax in your spacious room—just don't be surprised when a bull saunters past your window. Once a farm, always a farm.

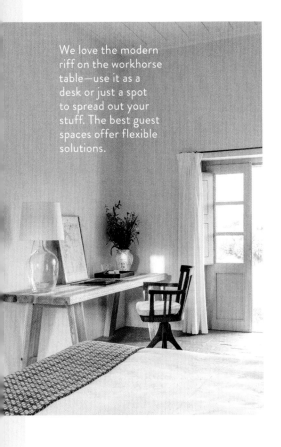

We love the modern riff on the workhorse table—use it as a desk or just a spot to spread out your stuff. The best guest spaces offer flexible solutions.

With views over fields and farms, this bathing beauty beckons you to take an afternoon soak while warm breezes waft in. Hold all calls!

A crisp and contemporary unfitted wood kitchen is rendered in a single material with smoky sage-green accents, thanks to a casual pantry and covetable director's chairs.

While away the days
lounging by the pool
or taking one of the
resort's horses for
a scenic ride.

The resort produces
its own wine from 37
acres of vineyards.

GRACE AFONSO   KAITLIN JOHNSON

SHARON BARR   JOHANNA
                    REYNOLDS
CHRISTINE FLYNN
                    HOLLY YOUNG

The Art of the Matter

We believe art and handmade elements are the soul of any home. In this issue, we're focusing on six women artists creating unique expressions for your walls at every price point.

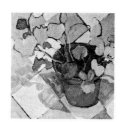

FROM TOP
So Early,
12" sq.
—
At a Friend's
Studio, 18" sq.
—
Table for Two,
30" sq.
—
Pink Cake Party,
24" sq.

GRACE AFONSO

Painter |
BUTTERGALLERY.CA

TRAINING GROUND

I've studied everywhere from the Haliburton School of the Arts to Perugia, Italy. The influential power of light and colour inspires me to be bold.

ONE COOL FACT

I paint from direct observation, so this means I can be found at the side of the road in all kinds of weather painting the perfect field scene or among the chaos of cake and presents at family birthday parties.

CREATIVE PROCESS

In plein air painting, I choose a view that captures my attention and I paint as quickly as I can before the light changes. In my studio, I set up a still life and make many changes to composition and colour until it expresses what I want.

PRICE RANGE

From $145 (6" sq.) to $1,950 (36" sq.).

CHRISTINE FLYNN

Photographer |
CHRISTINEFLYNNART.COM

INSPIRATION

My biggest inspiration comes from
travel. But really great design always
catches my eye—and I encounter both
on trips or my daily travels, whether it's
a coffee shop or boutique hotel lobby.

PREFERRED PALETTE

Nature dictates my palette; it always
starts there. I'm inspired by the muted
fog and mist of Southern California
surf, the rosé pink sunsets in Nosara,
and the unparalleled greens of Muskoka.

WHAT WORD DESCRIBES
YOUR WORK

Captivating, because it means the
images are engaging to others and that
each piece has the potential to create
a feeling for a person or space.

PRICE RANGE

From $3,400 (36" sq.) to $6,200
(72" x 42")

FROM TOP
Kommetjie Surfers,
60" x 36"
—
Manarola, 36" diam.
—
Valley of Fire State,
42" x 60"

JOHANNA REYNOLDS

Painter |
JOHANNAREYNOLDS.CA

CREATIVE PROCESS

My paintings are 70% in my head, so when I start to physically work on a piece, they usually burst out of me in a flurry before finding their own pace.

PREFERRED PALETTE

I love painting with Prussian blue, black, blush pink, ochre yellow, sap green, and chartreuse. I tend to start each painting with a big, dark abstracted shape and build around it.

ONE COOL FACT

In December 2018, Air Canada purchased four large paintings for their newly redesigned Maple Leaf lounge at LaGuardia Airport in New York. It's a huge honour and professional milestone to be part of their permanent collection!

PRICE RANGE

From $1,300 (24" x 20") to $5,500 (60" x 48")

CLOCKWISE
FROM TOP
Break/Through, 30" sq.
—
Bounty, 24" x 20"sq.
—
Gentle Air, 48" sq.
—
Alternate Routes,
60"x 48"

ARTIST SPOTLIGHT

CLOCKWISE
FROM TOP
Strawberry Cream,
42" sq.
—
Blue Boho, 50" sq.
—
Breath of the Wild,
54" sq.

KAITLIN JOHNSON

Painter |
KAITLIN-JOHNSON.COM

INSPIRATION

Inspiration comes from interior design, textiles, nature, or just seeing a certain combination of colours. Images and art from cultures around the world, as well as my experiences while travelling, are also a big inspiration.

PREFERRED PALETTE

I work with a lot of off-whites, creams, and pale pinks, because they impart a light and airy feeling. I accent this with hits of vibrant colour. Bright green is a favourite, and pink always seems to find its way into every piece.

ONE COOL FACT

I often break into dance when a song comes on that I'm really feeling while I'm painting—or any time, really!

PRICE RANGE

From $1,300 (36" sq.) to $3,000 (55" sq.)

HOLLY YOUNG

Mixed Media |
HOLLYYOUNGART.CA

INSPIRATION

I love mid-century architecture and seek to explore combinations that intrigue the senses and reveal the unexpected. The combination of lines, texture, and pattern inspire my work.

PREFERRED PALETTE

One month, I might explore a neutral colour palette on linen or canvas, then switch to textured mixed media collages on paper.

ONE COOL FACT

The titles of my pieces are often influenced by the music I was listening to while I was creating it.

PRICE RANGE

From $65 (4" x 6")
to $120 (8" x 10")

LEFT
Deco, 4" x 6"
—
BELOW
Road Block, 8" x 10"
(left), Stacked, 8" x 10"

SHARON BARR

Painter |
SHARONBARR.CA

CREATIVE PROCESS

My creative process begins by just making marks or throwing down a wash of colour and adding layers and marks until it makes rhythmical and visual sense to me.

ONE COOL FACT

My work is not all about perfection and beauty. I regularly self-edit, destroy the work, and start again. Risk-taking is a must for artistic evolution, so not everything has a happy ending.

WHAT WORD DESCRIBES
YOUR WORK

Can I use two? Visual poetry.

PRICE RANGE

From $4,200 (48" sq.) to $9,300 (72" sq.)

FROM TOP
Blue Escapism,
48" x 60"
—
Earth Vibrations I,
60" sq.
—
Earth Vibrations II,
60" sq.

ARTIST SPOTLIGHT

"BEING OUT HERE ON THE WEST DECK—FEELING THE BREEZE, LOOKING OVER THE EXPANSE OF OPEN WATER, AND LISTENING TO THE WAVES—IS ONE OF MY ALL-TIME FAVOURITE DESTINATIONS. WHEN THINGS GET CHAOTIC IN MY CITY LIFE, I VISUALIZE MYSELF HERE, UNPLUGGED, LIVING OFF THE GRID, AND FEELING CONNECTED TO NATURE."

—

On the Rocks

Out on the rugged open water of Georgian Bay, storm winds can blow up to 100 km/hr. Teak chairs weather to silvery grey and are heavy enough to not blow away.

DESIGN BY **SARAH RICHARDSON**
PHOTOGRAPHY BY **VALERIE WILCOX**

DESIGN BY
SARAH RICHARDSON,
SARAH RICHARDSON DESIGN

GEORGIAN BAY, ONTARIO

2,100 SQUARE FEET

12 MILES BY BOAT

4 BEDROOMS

1 BUNKIE

1.5 BATHS

2 DAUGHTERS

2 GUINEA PIGS

1 DOG

8 SOLAR PANELS

↑
A modern woven console table nests beneath a rustic mirror framed with straw hats and proves that when it comes to display at the cottage, you'll never go wrong in celebrating the simplicity of practical and useful items.

To maintain the natural grain of tongue-and-groove pine walls, a pale grey green latex paint was mixed with 50% water to achieve a light semitransparent wall finish. The original whitewash stain on rough-sawn pine ties to the warmth of white oak flooring.

↑
Island meals are a casual affair, so comfort and practicality are key when it comes to décor. The variegated blues in the end chairs and rug allude to the ever-changing blues on the lake, while the side chairs feature a two-textile mix—white leather on the seats for durability and a printed cotton on the backs for a bit of pattern. If more is more when it comes to the number of guests at your table, you can always build to suit. The dining table base is crafted from leftover barn wood and the top is made from standard builder lumber with a DIY stain finish.

The cottage runs on a north-south axis in the centre of a tiny island, so every view is almost like you're on a houseboat. The "storm room" is the main living room, facing south with three walls of windows and sliding doors out onto the deck.

TWENTY-ONE YEARS after the cottage was built as a bachelor cottage, and eleven years after it was renovated to accomodate growing family life with a toddler and a baby on the way, the remote off-the-grid island getaway of Sarah and her husband, Alexander Younger, got a final refresh to suit life with two tween/teen daughters (and frequent summer-season guests) on the rocks of Georgian Bay. It all started with a simple plan to enclose a screened-in porch and replace doors and windows that hadn't stood up to the exposed island location, but soon turned into an exercise in evaluating how to make the compact cottage live better for the future. The goal was to keep what worked and tweak what didn't, based on more than two decades of island life, both with and without kids.

← Vintage leaf-patterned ceramic lamps and wicker side tables flank a linen-covered sofa with a sculptural profile that nods to mid-century silhouettes. All the patterned fabrics evoke water-inspired patterns in rich blue hues. When working with colour, a little can go a long way, so all the upholstery and the rug are light natural cream tones that are as casually elegant as a linen shirt.

↓ When planning the furniture layout for a room with a dynamite view, the last thing you want to do is block it. A pair of chaises covered in washed linen keep the sight lines open and encourage those oh-so-important cottage life activites— spontaneous napping, daydreaming, and watching the clouds go by. The sweeping back profile and tailored legs keep the feeling spare in a room where airiness is the goal.

Cottage living rooms are where families and crowds gather. The vintage rattan chairs swivel into the room or out to the water. Two chaises, a deep and loungey sofa, a pair of clubby chairs, a couple of easy-to-move-anywhere ottomans, and a pair of cool vintage chairs are all anchored around an oversized vintage coffee table that's equal parts sentimental and indestructible.

DETAILS WE LOVE

1- Powered by solar panels, the cottage kitchen and dining room are illuminated by candlelight. Mounting lanterns on hooks amplifies the glow of the candles.

2- The Ming green and Thassos marble "sunflower" backsplash sparkles with the reflection of the late-afternoon sun on the lake for a truly "watery" feeling in the bar.

3- Seeded glass panels in the bar cupboards are filled with little air bubbles like a crashing wave or a chilled glass of champagne.

4- The multicolour cabinetry in the kitchen features an accent of robin's egg blue framing salvaged painted panelling from an 1860's schoolhouse.

Upper Cabinet Colour:
Gray Cashmere (2138-60) by Benjamin Moore

Island Colour:
Wedgewood Gray (HC-146) by Benjamin Moore

→

Building a cottage on a rugged granite island demands that you work with the landscape and adapt your building accordingly. A giant section of lichen-covered rock rises above counter height just outside the bar windows and provides a seamless connection between indoors and out.

"The surrounding water landscape changes constantly with the weather and time of day—there's no singular 'lake blue.' There are a thousand shades, and those variations in palette make each space feel a little bit different from the next."

—Sarah Richardson

←

Having the chance to rethink and redecorate the interior after a decade lets you keep the things you love and tweak the things you don't to make the most of every area. What used to be a combined dining room and sitting area is now just an expansive airy dining room with a 10-foot table to accomodate big cottage dinners with family, friends, and guests.

↑

The fireplace in the porch is a woodstove designed to generate maximum heat when it's needed most, while the elevated firebox allows the flames to be enjoyed from across the room. The cottage sits on a granite island, and the marble surround was chosen for the sinuous veins and subdued palette that complements the greyed floor tone.

→

Once a screened porch, this room is now a fully enclosed, weatherproof indoor room—yet it still feels as open and airy as ever with the doors and windows wide open. Vinyl plank floors mix with chunky wood and wicker accents for a room that is intended for laid-back, feet-up living.

"Cottage life is about picnics, boat adventures, and outdoor pleasures—who wants to fuss about the furniture? The giant sectional sofa is made up of stock pieces with washable white cotton slipcovers. Instead of arms, the two ends feature armless, backless ottoman components with hidden storage." —SR

←
Without a basement
(or an abundance of
extra room), a spot
for the laundry room
had to be carved
out of whatever
space was available.
What was once a
roof deck became
an enclosed laundry
area between and
beneath two roof
peaks—handily
tucked behind sliding
barn doors made
from renovation
leftovers.

→
Thirteen-year-old
Robin got to design
the direction of her
bedroom once she
no longer shared it
with a little sister.
The mint stripe was
a feature in the
original bedroom.
It's now the only
accent of colour
amidst a wispy-soft
palette of white and
pale grey that—along
with the upper-floor
location and ethereal
scrunched paper
pendant lights above
the bed—makes
you feel as if you're
floating in the
clouds.

↑
With compact proportions and high traffic, the focus is on simple, natural materials. The freestanding tub sits beneath a skylight and floats in front of a textured chisel-face marble wall. Instead of towel bars, lots of modern marble hooks make it easy to hang up soggy towels. The honed marble floor feels cottage-appropriate thanks to dramatic grey-green veining reminiscent of patterns on the water. A simple round white mirror and bubbly glass pendant light add softness to the bathroom by breaking up the boxy silhouettes.

"Painted floors remind me of the cottages I grew up in. There's no better feeling than bare feet on a painted floor in summer. Whitewashed furniture with chunky round knobs, softened silhouettes, and tapered legs feel contemporary but have the relaxed sunwashed look of cottage life." —SR

↓
The principal bedroom's palette harnesses the serenity of the shore as it melts into the lake. Washed grey linen window coverings and pillows combined with denim blues, pale wood, and contemporary lighting make for a simply spare weekend retreat.

YES, YOU CAN!

Inject extra personality by sanding and painting hardwood floors in a two-hued stripe.
Step 1: Paint the entire floor in the lighter colour.
Step 2: Use painter's masking tape and add a few stripes in a slightly darker tone.

←
The bunkie was born the same time as Sarah's younger daughter, Fiona, and offers an escape from the main cottage. What it lacks in square footage, due to compact proportions and zoning regulations, it makes up for with expansive views over the water. Tommy nicknamed the location "Ether Island" for the deep sleeps he enjoys here.

↑
The best guest spaces offer everything you need and nothing you don't: a comfy bed, soft sheets and pillows, extra blankets, surfaces to spread out on, a desk to stay connected, a chair to flop on, and no extraneous clutter. This compact bedroom sits across the lawn from the cottage at the water's edge. The fabrics are reminiscent of summer sails, while the lacquered bedside tables feature a carved wave detail—both subtle references to the lakeside location without being "theme-y" or contrived.

↓
On Georgian Bay, the local vernacular dictates that cottages blend in discreetly with the natural surroundings instead of shouting, "Look at me!" The window and trim colour is called "Midnight Surf," which feels entirely appropriate for the rocky setting and allows the windows to disappear in the long building that runs along a north/south axis, flooding the entire structure with light all day long.

↓
Running the entire length of the cottage from north to south, the east-facing deck looks out to the main harbour and provides a sunny spot to lounge in the wind shadow of the prevailing north and west winds. The loungers, which combine aluminum frames with recycled plastic slats, wheel easily to chase shade or sun.

↑
The genius of juxtaposing a boldly modern Miró against rustic log walls creates a major aha moment. Country style is at its best when it includes the element of surprise.

French Accent

"A FARMHOUSE SHOULD BE SOULFUL. IT CANNOT BE PERFECT OR PRISTINE; IT'S ABOUT EASY LIVING, AND SHOULD FEEL INVITING AND WARM—AN APPLE PIE OF A HOUSE!"

DESIGN BY RICHARD OUELLETTE & MAXIME VANDAL

PHOTOGRAPHY BY ANDRÉ RIDER

DESIGN BY
**RICHARD
OUELLETTE
AND MAXIME
VANDAL,** LES
ENSEMBLIERS

HEMMINGFORD,
QUEBEC

4,500 SQUARE
FEET

300 YEARS OLD

160 ACRE
PROPERTY

5 BEDROOMS

5 BATHROOMS

1.5-YEAR
RENOVATION

→
Oak millwork, plaid upholstery, and leather accents give the mudroom that Scottish Highlands feeling in the Quebec countryside. "This wood felt natural and pure with a contemporary touch in a home that had every type of wood, from B.C. fir to old cedar," says Richard.

HOW DO YOU make a 300-year-old Quebec farmhouse feel like it's been dropped into the Scottish Highlands? Just ask Richard Ouellette and Maxime Vandal of Montreal design firm Les Ensembliers. They restored and renovated the 18th-century estate's two buildings—a stone house and two-storey barn—before layering in soft colours and cozy textiles to give their clients a getaway with soul. "I paired winter and summer fabrics together as if people just added to it over the years," says Richard. "We intentionally didn't try to come up with a 'palette' because if we matched things together, it wouldn't look authentic." The goal was always to reflect how the family lives today—with plenty of gatherings and al fresco dinners—while respecting the property's history. "This wasn't just a checklist of all the clients' design dreams—of all the Pinterest likes in one place. This was a collaboration with an old structure. You really have to lean into what the structure says instead of jamming all your dreams inside it," says Maxime.

↓
Don't be afraid to
make the back of a
peninsula work hard
with added storage
and display for
cookbooks.

←
Contemporary art
and lighting add
edge to the rustic
kitchen; the strong
black accents are the
perfect counterpoint
to soft blue-greys
and pale wood tones.

Cabinet colour:
Oilcloth (CSP-76) by
Benjamin Moore

"We asked if we could place
the Mirós in the kitchen and
the client, a true collector, said,
'Of course, why not?' He believes
art should be enjoyed."

—Richard Ouellette

YES, YOU CAN!
Break symmetry with a pendant that angles to one side.

DETAILS WE LOVE

1- Unfitted cabinetry gives a nod to historic European kitchens.

2- Wooden cooking utensils become art when hung across a simple dowel.

3- A butcher-block worktable on casters can be rolled into action and looks airy.

4- White oak floors in a chevron pattern add a touch of modern sophistication.

This next-level kitchen table concept—mixing chairs with a bench, and bookending it with shelving—embodies everything that's delightful about farmhouse living.

"We envisioned a place built over time:
Pieces that didn't match, finishes that
were imperfect, and fabrics that mixed
plaids and florals." —RO

← Putty-toned walls create a warm, neutral backdrop for rich fabrics. "Richard pushed for leaving the faded, crumbling plaster walls," says Maxime. "The colours drafted off that." The art displayed in the home doesn't share a period or story line—it's just a collection of pieces the homeowners love.

Celebrate what you've got, whether it's rustic beams or a raised tub. With the right imagination, challenges become design highlights.

YES, YOU CAN!
Install a sliding barn door with a twist to give a modern accent to a rustic space.

←
Intersecting lines in the ceiling, artwork, and barn door give the lounge adjacent to the master bedroom a gallery vibe.

↑
Tactile elements are important—and nothing's better than falling into a bed made up with touchable fabrics after a day of fresh air.

"BALANCE THE BEST OF WHAT YOU STARTED WITH AND INFUSE IT WITH NEW ENERGY AND IDEAS."

→ You don't need fancy tools to design your culinary masterpiece. The entire layout for the kitchen of *Sarah Off the Grid* season 2 was sketched in a spiral notebook while on a plane. If you can "blue sky" dream it, you can build it.

Nouveau Victorian

YES, YOU CAN!

Customize in-store cabinetry with solid wood surrounds to act as gables. It's easy, inexpensive, and yet looks bespoke.

DESIGN BY **SARAH RICHARDSON**

INTERIOR PHOTOGRAPHY BY **STACEY BRANDFORD**

EXTERIOR PHOTOGRAPHY BY **VALERIE WILCOX**

DESIGN BY
SARAH RICHARDSON,
SARAH RICHARDSON DESIGN

CREEMORE, ONTARIO

2,000 SQUARE FEET

116 YEARS OLD

4 BEDROOMS

2.5 BATHROOMS

25 NEW WINDOWS

8-MONTH RENOVATION

1 TV SHOW

WHEN SARAH TOURED the Victorian home, a potential location for season 2 of her show, *Sarah Off the Grid*, it was love at first site visit. Though the house had been cared for and lived in, with plenty of historical charm and character intact throughout, it was ripe for a renovation. "It was the type of house you'd see from the street, pause, and smile—a classic diamond in the rough," says Sarah. "She was already pretty, she just needed a makeover." The house was also situated on a third of an acre and had a barn, and all this right in the middle of a quaint small town. Sarah jumped at the chance to refresh the home indoors and out, and replace the "handyman special" addition with a contemporary space that added two more bedrooms, a living room, and an extra one-and-a-half baths. Now ready to meet the needs of modern family life, the diamond in the rough was sparkling once again.

↑
Changing the exterior trim elements from cream to deep graphite grey gives the historic façade a more contemporary appearance while creating a cohesive connection to the modern addition.

→
Curb appeal is de rigeur in any renovation, but don't overlook the back of the house. The linear addition was clad in 1" x 12" rough-sawn barn boards that were pre-stained before install to make the new building feel at home with the original house and barn. A slatted panel screen performs double duty as a privacy barrier and backdrop for the outdoor "room."

YES, YOU CAN!
Choose anything but basic white when placing an order for custom vinyl windows— there are dozens of pre-painted colours available.

"A kitchen is like a puzzle, and a good layout is the key to success."
—Sarah Richardson

DETAILS WE LOVE

1- Geometric pendants raise the bar on task lighting.

2- Slatted detailing on the vent hood turns a functional piece into a design feature.

3- A slab marble backsplash is a splurge but saves on tile installation costs.

4- The dual-height island hides a servery and creates a barrier to the open dining room.

Cabinet colour:
Lakefront (90BG 31/124) by Dulux

↓
The dining room is a stylish yet comfortable place to gather with family and friends, so it was designed with big groups and small (and messy) diners in mind—the chairs are upholstered in vinyl for wipe-clean ease. On the wall, iPhone images were mounted in ready-made frames for a super-easy DIY.

→

SUBTLE MOMENTS

The mudroom packs a lot of punch for a tiny entry. The half wall was clad in a geometric pattern using thin strips of poplar wood installed in four different directions.

→

Low-hung art is an unexpected touch at the base of the stairs, drawing the eye up to the second storey.

YES, YOU CAN!
Paint just the stair treads dark but leave the risers, spindles, and handrail light.

↓

Texture and tone-on-tone pattern make an all-grey room feel cozy (a roaring fire doesn't hurt, either). Vintage rattan chairs repainted in charcoal grey, a sleek marble mantel, and mirrors in a beehive configuration add contemporary appeal.

→

Soft greys rule in this neutral living room, giving way to a few crisp black-and-white accessories for contrast and impact. A cream rug, printed linen drapes, and oodles of natural light bring in all the warmth needed to keep these cool tones from feeling cold.

YES, YOU CAN!

Keep the TV hidden from view when not in use with a series of framed photographs connected with piano hinges to act as retractable doors.

"Looking out to the weathered boards on the barn while sitting in the addition make the two buildings feel connected. And while I love colour, sometimes the calm of no colour plays well in a contemporary space." –SR

YES, YOU CAN!

Paint a vintage find
in a fearless colour.

BOLD
BEDROOMS

What to do with an angled ceiling? Run the wallpaper up the wall, across the ceiling, and back down the other side. Matching DIY headboards, bedding, and reading lights calm the effect of the wallpaper's energetic print.

↓

Inspired by the rich red buds of the sumac trees, the rusty orange accents of this bedroom are a natural extension of the Victorian red-brick exterior of this century charmer. Salvaged arrows hung above the bed inject a sense of fun.

Dresser Colour:
Autumn Crisp
(70GY 30/254) by
ICI/Dulux

Attention to detail makes the principal bathroom sing. Tall mirrors echo the height of the slim window behind the tub, while a waterfall edge dresses up the vanity counter. Cement tiles can be installed in a multitude of configurations (like this zigzag pattern), allowing you to put your personal stamp on the floor.

"The original fieldstone foundation we unearthed during construction became the palette inspiration for the media room." —SR

↓
Skip the drywall in a basement room in favour
of shiplap-style plywood panelling. It's durable,
it's easy to install, and it adds to the rustic appeal.

YES, YOU CAN!

Use stock
butcher-block
counters to make a
waterfall edge for
a folding counter
and appliance
surround.

Uncovering hidden potential is one of the most exciting elements of design. The original working barn, built circa 1904, was cleared of junk and turned into a clubhouse entertaining destination.

Twinkle lights create a festive mood for an al fresco dinner party inside the barn. Scoop-back chairs and a table made from two vintage sawhorses work as no-fuss furnishings. Simply add food and drink, and let the summer good times begin!

"IT'S RARE TO EXPERIENCE A HOUSE THIS STATELY THAT SITS SO CLOSE TO THE CRASHING WAVES. AS SOON AS WE SAW IT IN PERSON, WE KNEW EXACTLY WHAT IT NEEDED."

With the kitchen garden just outside, a humble pegboard holds hats and coats instead of hiding them in a cupboard. "Sometimes, a bit of mess is intrinsic and a little bit of imperfection is the perfect thing," says Tommy.

Coastal Colonial

DESIGN BY TOMMY SMYTHE & LINDSAY MENS CRAIG

PHOTOGRAPHY BY VIRGINIA MACDONALD

DESIGN BY
**TOMMY SMYTHE
& LINDSAY
MENS CRAIG,**
SARAH
RICHARDSON
DESIGN

LONG ISLAND
SOUND,
CONNECTICUT

7,000 SQUARE
FEET

19TH CENTURY

8 BEDROOMS

7 BATHROOMS

6 FIREPLACES

3 RENOVATION
PHASES OVER
3 YEARS

**YES,
YOU CAN!**

Avoid potlights
when they don't
feel right for
the home's age
and go with
classic flush-
mount fixtures
instead.

> "The clients wanted a white kitchen and the house seemed to want that, too. The goal was to make it look like it had been this way since the twenties."
>
> —Tommy Smythe

→

In a house with eight bedrooms and seven bathrooms, the kitchen needs to work hard, and this one does—there's two of everything, but all appliances are hidden by panel-fronts to keep the look authentic.

←

Hand-glazed subway tiles installed to the ceiling help transition from the kitchen's open work space to the more formal living areas. Bonus: Their texture and shimmer feel period-specific. "It wouldn't be a big stretch to imagine these tiles were made locally in 1922," says Tommy.

SOME PEOPLE WOULD step inside a seafront clapboard house and see the grand columns and staircase. Designer Tommy Smythe saw all that, but also imagined a woman wearing the wrong outfit. "I just felt that everything décor-wise wasn't flattering to the house. It had been well and properly renovated in the eighties, but there were some cues that weren't authentic," he says. When the client contacted the firm, the brief was simple: Make her fall back in love with the house—a getaway that was important to her husband but where she'd struggled to feel at home. Tommy and Lindsay Mens Craig reoriented all the furniture to take advantage of the views. Next, they had to strip the home of some of its formality. "Everything formal was given an informal treatment, and everything informal was dressed up a little," he says. So the damask upholstery on a settee was replaced with coarse linen, and a weathered antique trunk was topped with a fine, filigreed porcelain vase. Finding the right mix of casual and sophisticated was the ultimate key to comfort—and a reignited love affair with this home by the sea.

↑

White denim sofas and an antique steamer trunk make the living room less formal and more a place to put your feet up. "All the fabrics we picked are either cotton or linen, and all the wood finishes are a bit rustic," says Lindsay.

↓
When the dining room's an indoor-outdoor space, forgo the rugs and treat the floor to some slate tiles—perfect for high-traffic areas. A subtle seafaring mural, oversized lantern, and sunny accents make it an easygoing gathering place.

↓
Dark slate grasscloth cozies up a den that's flooded with natural light. When choosing something for over the mantel, look for a one-of-a-kind piece. The antique wood shell speaks to the kind of craftsmanship found throughout the home, as well as its waterfront location.

"The clients are mad about stripes, so of course we just had to add a striped wallpaper or fabric in every room as a signature flourish." —TS

YES, YOU CAN!

Don't be afraid to get moody, even in an oceanside home—as long as it's temperd with plenty of light-toned elements, the space will still feel airy and bright.

↑
Look-at-me wallpaper, a luxe yet subdued mirror that's elegant without being over-the-top, and a showstopper vanity converted from an antique Sheraton-style bowfront sideboard gives a powder room a sense of arrival. The sideboard was already stripped raw; Tommy and Lindsay decided to leave it that way rather than lacquer it, which would only darken the finish.

← A sophisticated nod to nautical style comes from the marine-blue-painted vanity and brass sconces.

↑
PRETTY IN PINK

Pink doesn't need to read as sweet. When used as an impactful accent in a bedroom that's tempered and grounded in neutral grey and cream, even the most traditional elements and patterns feel fresh and light.

←
Classic Fornasetti wallpaper references the area's stormy skies in a way that's sophisticated, not twee. "It's shocking when you see it go up, but when you dress the space, art and furnishings temper the effect," says Tommy.

"The female homeowner loves blue, and this room is my love letter to her. Big gestures in a tiny space give people permission to be themselves."

—T S

DETAILS WE LOVE

1- Adhering to a monochromatic scheme takes discipline. Start with a "hero" fabric (in this case, the floral) and layer in more graphic and geometric patterns in varying scales for a laid-back vibe.

2- A collection of plates on the wall looks curated over time, whether or not they were. This wall started with a few plates from the client and the rest were added for instant impact.

3- A French mattress was commissioned for the bed in a casual woven fabric.

4- Fun floral prints in cobalt and sky blue feel like a classic Chinese ginger jar.

DESIGNER DIRECTORY
(In order of appearance)

Sarah Richardson Design
sarahrichardsondesign.com

Sophie Burke Design
sophieburkedesign.com

Chango & Co.
chango.co

Nam Dang-Mitchell Design
namdangmitchell.com

Feasby & Bleeks Design
feasbyandbleeks.com

Les Ensembliers
ensembliers.com

"HERITAGE CLASSIC," pages 4 to 19
BREAKFAST ROOM Kravet: roman blind fabric, **kravet.com** | Design Within Reach: table, chairs, **dwr.com** | Rich Brilliant Willing: chandelier, **richbrilliantwilling.com** | Saltillo Imports: floor tile, **saltillo-tiles.com**.

EXTERIOR Benjamin Moore: exterior, Forest Green (HC-187); front door, Ravishing Red (2008-10); porch floor, Chelsea Gray (HC-168); **benjaminmoore.com**.

ENTRYWAY Elte: stair runner, **elte.com** | Rich Brilliant Willing: sconces, **richbrilliantwilling.com**.

LIVING ROOM Sarah Richardson Design: sofa, ottoman, upholstered chair, **sarahrichardsondesign.com** | Memo: large pillow accent fabric, **memoshowroom.com** | Design Within Reach: wood-framed chair, coffee table, stool, **dwr.com** | Kravet: sofa fabric, accent fabrics, upholstered chair fabric, ottoman fabric, Lee Jofa roman blind fabric, Christopher Farr wallpaper, **kravet.com** | Royal Antique Rug Gallery: rug, **rarg.ca** | Ciot: fireplace marble, **ciot.com** | Dinuovo Granite & Marble Inc.: fireplace fabrication, **905-660-9910**.

DINING ROOM Kravet: drapery fabric, Christopher Farr wallpaper, **kravet.com** | Patina Antiques: dining table, console table, **patinaantiques.ca** | Sarah Richardson Design: dining chairs, **sarahrichardsondesign.com** | Schumacher: dining chair fabric, **fschumacher.com** | Bungalow 5: sideboard, **bungalow5.com** | Kathy Richardson: artwork, **kathyrichardsonphotography.ca** | Residential Lighting Studio: chandelier, **residentiallightingstudio.com**.

KITCHEN Sarah Richardson Design: counter stools, **sarahrichardsondesign.com** | Saltillo Imports: floor tiles, backsplash, **saltillo-tiles.ca** | Upper Canada Specialty Hardware: cabinetry hardware, **ucshshowroom.com** | Residential Lighting Studio: pendant lights, **residentiallightingstudio.com** | Tasco Appliances: appliances, **tascoappliance.ca** | Vent-A-Hood: vent hood, **ventahood.com** | Kravet: roman blind fabric, Lee Jofa counter stool fabric, **kravet.com** | Taps Bath Centre: sink, faucet, **tapsbath.com**.

LAUNDRY ROOM Tasco Appliances: washer, dryer, **tascoappliancc.ca** | Taps Bath Centre: Blanco sink, Rubinet faucet, **tapsbath.com** | Restoration Hardware: cabinet hardware, **restorationhardware.com** | Saltillo Imports: backsplash, floor tile, **saltillo-tiles.com**.

"MID-CENTURY MARVEL," pages 20 to 31
GENERAL Blackfish Homes: build, **blackfishhomes.ca** | Shelter Residential Design: architect, **buildshelter.com** | Capital Millwork: millwork, **capitalmillwork.ca** | Eckowood: engineered wood flooring, **eckowood.com**.

LIVING ROOM Enviro: fireplace, **enviro.com** | Herman Miller: pendants, **hermanmiller.com** | Van Gogh Designs: sofa, **vangoghdesigns.com** | Salari: area rug, **salari.com**.

POWDER ROOM Cedar & Moss: sconce, **cedarandmoss.com** | Caesarstone: countertop, **caesarstone.ca** | Schoolhouse: cabinet hardware, **schoolhouse.com** | Marrakech Design: tile, **marrakechdesign.se** | By Design Modern: mirror, **bydesignmodern.com** | Hansgrohe: faucet, **hansgrohe.com** | Blu Bathworks: sink, **blubathworks.com**.

PRINCIPAL BEDROOM Brendan Ravenhill: pendant, **brendanravenhill.com** | By Design Modern: night stands, **bydesignmodern.com**.

PRINCIPAL EN SUITE Cedar & Moss: pendants, **cedarandmoss.com** | Caesarstone: countertop, **caesarstoneus.com** | Schoolhouse: cabinetry hardware, **schoolhouse.com** | Hansgrohe: faucet, **hansgrohe.com** | Valley Acrylic Bath Ltd.: tub, **valleyacrylic.com** | Vintage Tub & Bath: tub filler, **vintagetub.com**.

KITCHEN Wolf: range, **ca.subzero-wolf.com** | Gaggenau: hood fan, **gaggenau.com** | Fisher & Paykel: double ovens, **fisherpaykel.com** | Liebherr: fridge, freezer, **home.liebherr.com** | Caesarstone: countertop, **caesarstoneus.com** | Ames Tile & Stone: backsplash, **amestile.com** | Franke: sink, **franke.com** | Blanco: faucet, **blanco.com**.

DINING ROOM Louis Poulsen: pendants, **louispoulsen.com**.

"URBAN COTTAGE," pages 32 to 43
LIVING ROOM Sarah Richardson Design: chairs, sofa, striped throw, **sarahrichardsondesign.com** | Patina Antiques: stools, **patinaantiques.ca** | Kelly Wearstler: stool fabric, **kellywearstler.com** | Vintage Fine Objects: chairs, coffee table, side tables, chandelier, mirror, **vintagefineobjects.com** | Kravet: Lee Jofa chair fabric, **kravet.com** | Dartford Home Inc.: lamps, **416-487-0667** | Woven Treasures: area rug, **416-943-0538** | Canvas Gallery: artwork, **canvasgallery.ca** |

Y&Co: cushions, ycocarpet.com | Thibaut: grasscloth wallpaper, thibautdesign.com.

ENTRYWAY Saltillo Imports: mosaic marble tiles, saltillo-tiles.com | Farrow & Ball: wallpaper, farrow-ball.com | Wesley Seto Designs: roman blind fabrication, 416-538-3223 | Sarah Richardson for Kravet: roman blind fabric, sarahrichardsondesign.com | Kravet: seat cushion fabric, kravet.com | Y&Co: pillow fabrics, ycocarpet.com | Vintage Fine Objects: coat rack, vintagefineobjects.com | Jacaranda Tree & Co.: lantern light fixture, 416-482-6599.

KITCHEN Ikea: cabinetry, appliances, cabinetry hardware, shelf tops, ikea.com | The Door Store: pendant lights, custom sconces, thedoorstore.ca | Caesarstone: countertops, caesarstone.ca | Saltillo Imports: backsplash, floor tiles, saltillo-tiles.com | Sarah Richardson Design: stools, sarahrichardsondesign.com | Anthropologie: shelf brackets, anthropologie.com.

FAMILY ROOM Sarah Richardson Design: ottoman, sofas, sarahrichardsondesign.com | Vintage Fine Objects: lamp, vintagefineobjects.com | Residential Lighting Studio: lantern light fixture, residentiallightingstudio.com | Canvas Gallery: artwork, canvasgallery.ca.

KENNEDY'S BEDROOM Around the Block: area rug, side lamps, aroundtheblock.com | Residential Lighting Studio: chandelier, residentiallightingstudio.com | Sarah Richardson Design: bed, sarahrichardsondesign.com | Annie Selke: Pine Cone Hill duvet cover, annieselke.com | Kravet: Lee Jofa wallpaper, kravet.com | Allan Rug Co.: flooring, allanrug.com.

NURSERY Elte Market: area rug, eltemkt.com | Wesley Seto Designs: roman blind fabrication, 416-538-3223 | Sarah Richardson Design: chair, sarahrichardsondesign.com | Y&Co: toss pillow fabric, stool fabric, ycocarpet.com | Ikea: crib, ikea.com | Jacaranda Tree & Co.: table, 416-482-6599 | Châtelet: bookcase, chatelethome.com | Kravet: Lee Jofa wallpaper, kravet.com.

PRINCIPAL BEDROOM Sarah Richardson Design: bed, sarahrichardsondesign.com | Vintage Fine Objects: lamp, vintagefine-objects.com | Woven Treasures: area rug, 416-943-0538 | Residential Lighting Studio: chandelier, residentiallightingstudio.com | Eglin Picture & Frame: framing, elginpictureandframe.com | Around the Block: chair, aroundtheblock.com | Eclectisaurus: artwork, eclectisaurus.com | Ellie Cashman: pillow fabric, elliecashmandesign.com.

BATHROOM Restoration Hardware: vanity hardware, restorationhardware.com | The Rubinet Faucet Company: faucets, rubinet.com | Elgin Picture & Frame: custom mirrors, elginpictureandframe.com | Union Lighting & Furnishings: pendant lights, unionlightingandfurnishings.com | Residential Lighting Studio: sconce, residentiallightingstudio.com | Saltillo Imports: marble mosaic flooring, saltillo-tiles.com.

"STYLE FACTORY," pages 44 to 57
LIVING ROOM Croft House: Bronson console, crofthouse.com | Stark Carpet: custom rug, starkcarpet.com | Tom Dixon: side table, tomdixon.net | Desiron: lounge chairs, desiron.com | Haute Living: stools, hauteliving.com | Restoration Hardware: Parisian track arm sofa, restorationhardware.com | Azulina Home: pillows, azulina.com.

DINING NOOK Palecek: chandelier, palecek.com | Design Within Reach: dining table, dwr.com | Chango Shop: mudcloth stripe pillow, in cream and black, chango.shop.

KITCHEN Blu Dot: chip leather barstool, bludot.com | Chango Shop: accessories, chango.shop | Circa Lighting: konos pendant, circalighting.com.

ENTRYWAY 1st Dibs: KG console table, 1stdibs.com | Restoration Hardware: metal floating mirror, restorationhardware.com | Chango Shop: large round seagrass basket, chango.shop.

PLAY AREA Century House: hanging Cee chairs, centuryhouseinc.com | Duc Duc: Parker playtable, ducducnyc.com | Flor: carpet tiles, flor.com.

PRINCIPAL BEDROOM Bernhardt: Palma canopy bed, bernhardt.com | Shades of Light: grooved concrete table lamps, small, shadesoflight.com | Chango Shop: bench, Ina mudcloth pillow, in natural, chango.shop.

BOY'S BEDROOM Leslee Mitchell: artwork, lesleemitchellart.com | Serena & Lily: feather wallpaper in denim, serenaandlily.com | Restoration Hardware: Cole house trundle bed, restorationhardware.com.

GIRL'S BEDROOM Brewster Home Fashions: wallpaper, brewsterwallcovering.com | Kinder Modern: stool, kindermodern.com | Uprise Art: artwork, upriseart.com | Restoration Hardware: glider, ceiling pendant, restorationhardware.com.

KIDS' BATHROOM Studio Four NYC: wallpaper, studiofournyc.com | Serena & Lily: French tassel shower curtain, serenaandlily.com.

"ON THE ROCKS," pages 74 to 93
GENERAL Martin Windows: doors and windows, fenetresmartin.com | Muskoka Lumber: tongue-and-groove panelling, muskokalumber.ca | Cape Cod Siding: finished

wood siding, **capecodsiding.com** | Fiber & Cloth: flooring, **fiberandcloth.com**.

DINING ROOM Sarah Richardson Design: chairs, napkins, **sarahrichardsondesign.com** | Kravet: Kelly Wearstler dining chair fabric, **kravet.com** | Premier Prints: dining chair fabric, **premierprintsinc.com** | Perfect Leather Goods Ltd. leather seat fabric, perfectleathergoods.com | Tonic Living: drapery fabric, **tonicliving.com** | Wayfair: fireplace mirror, mirror above console, wicker console table, plates and bowls, **wayfair.ca** | Loloi: rug, **loloirugs.com** | Ikea: wicker basket, **ikea.com** | CB2: white geo bowls, white bowls on wicker console, **cb2.ca** | Simon Pearce: candlesticks, **simonpearce.com** | A. H. Wilkens Auctions & Appraisals: linen covered console, **ahwilkens.com**.

LIVING ROOM Sarah Richardson Design: chaises, sofa, chairs, grey throws, **sarahrichardsondesign.com** | Kravet: accent pillow fabrics, **kravet.com** | Premier Prints: chaise fabric, sofa fabric, rattan chair cushion covers, **premierprintsinc.com** | Tonic Living: drapery fabric, **tonicliving.com** | Wayfair: side tables by chaises, **wayfair.ca** | CB2: Orville poufs, large and small vases, **cb2.com** | Miller Island Company: rattan swivel chairs, rattan side table, **millerislandcompany .com** | Eclectisaurus: blue-rimmed bowl, **eclectisaurus.com** | Of Things Past: side tables, **ofthingspast.com** | Dinuovo Granite & Marble: side table marble tops, **905-660-9910** | Penney & Co.: lamps, **penneyandcompanyhome.com** | Benjamin Moore: paint, Gray Owl (OC-52), **benjaminmoore.com**.

KITCHEN Saltillo Tiles: marble mosaic backsplash, **saltillo-tiles.com** | Sarah Richardson Design: counter stools, **sarahrichardsondesign.com** | Perfect Leather Goods Ltd.: leather stool fabric, **perfectleathergoods.com** | Legacy Vintage: corbels and panelling, **legacyvintage.ca** | Caesarstone: countertop, **caesarstone.ca** | Tasco Appliances: Fisher & Paykel dishwasher drawer, bar fridge, **tascoappliance.ca** | Blanco: kitchen sink, bar sink, **blanco.com** | The Rubinet Faucet Company: bar sink faucet, **rubinet.com** | Hansgrohe: kitchen sink faucet, **hansgrohe.com** | Northern Living Kitchen & Bath Ltd.: cabinetry, **northernlivingkitchenandbath.ca** | The Door Store: cabinetry hardware, **thedoorstore.ca** | Ikea: task lamp, **ikea.com** | Wayfair: Sophie Conran bowls and dinnerware, **wayfair.ca** | Vintage Fine Objects: white planters, **vintagefineobjects.com** | CB2: white vase, **cb2.com** | Benjamin Moore: cabinetry paint, Wedgewood Gray (HC-146), Gray Cashmere (2138-60), November Rain (2142-60), **benjaminmoore.com**.

PORCH Pacific Energy: wood stove, **pacificenergy.net**, through Fireplace & Leisure Centre, **fplc.ca** | New Age Granite & Marble: marble slabs for wood stove, **newagegranite**

.com | Dinuovo Granite & Marble Inc.: marble fabrication, **905-660-9910** | Ikea: sofa, storage cabinetry, **ikea.com** | Richelieu: brass knobs, **richelieu.com**, through Lowe's, **lowes.ca** | Wayfair: lamp, wicker chairs, wicker side tables, twist side table, loungers, planters, **wayfair.ca** | Elle & Eve: coffee table, **elleandeve.ca** | The Miller Island Company: pendant, **millerislandcompany.com** | Kravet: pillow fabrics, Kravet Basics, Lee Jofa, **kravet.com** | Pottery Barn: brass task lamp, **potterybarn.ca** | Rona: tongue-and-groove panelling on ceiling and walls, **rona.ca** | Tuuci: patio umbrellas, **tuuci.com**.

LAUNDRY Wayfair: white towels, wicker baskets with stripes, **wayfair.ca** | Tonic Living: drapes on the door to the laundry room, **tonicliving.ca** | Lowes: barn door assembly, **lowes.ca** | Sarah Richardson Design: tea towels, **sarahrichardsondesign.com**.

BATHROOM Wayfair: towels, ceramic stool, **wayfair.ca** | Dezign Market: vanity, **dezignmarket.com** | Ikea: mirror, **ikea.com** | Arteriors: pendant, **arteriorshome.com** | Saltillo Tiles: floor, shower, mosaic wall tiles, **saltillo-tiles.com** | The Rubinet Faucet Company: shower system, tub filler, vanity faucet, **rubinet.com** | Taps Bath: Passion tub, **tapsbath.com** | American Standard: toilet, **americanstandard.ca** | Adanac Glass: shower enclosure, **adanacglass.com** | Legacy Vintage Building Materials & Antiques: cabinet over tub, **legacyvintage.ca** | Velux: skylight, **velux.ca**.

ROBIN'S BEDROOM Ikea: mirror, pendant lamps, desk cabinets, and butcher block, **ikea .com** | Kravet: accent pillow fabic, **kravet.com** | Sarah Richardson for Kravet: accent pillow fabric, **sarahrichardsondesign.com** | Tonic Living: accent pillow fabric, **tonicliving.ca** | Premier Prints: headboard fabric, roman blind fabric, **premierprintsinc.com** | Zara Home: duvet cover, **zarahome.com** | Benjamin Moore: nightstand paint, Whitestone (2134-60), **benjaminmoore.com**.

PRINCIPAL BEDROOM Wayfair: fan, grey lamp, cement side tables, dresser, round mirror, side tables, woven basket, wall mount lamps (Louis Poulsen), door stopper, **wayfair.ca** | Sarah Richardson Design: chairs, bedding, **sarahrichardsondesign.com** | Sarah Richardson for Kravet: chair fabric, chair pillow fabric, **sarahrichardsondesign.com** | Kravet: headboard fabric, **kravet.com** | Elgin Picture: "framing, **elginpictureandframe.com** | Audubon: "Birds of America" print digital download, **audubon.org** | Toronto Image Works: printing of Audubon bird, **torontoimageworks.com** | CB2: wall mount bar with throw, **www.cb2.ca** | Tonic Living: window drape fabric, **tonicliving.ca** | Elte Mkt: bed throw pillow, **eltemkt.com** | McNabb Home Building Centre: hardwood floors, **mcnabblumber.ca** | CIL: wall paint, White on White (30GY 88/014), floor paint, Faded Denim (10BB 55/065), **cil.ca**.

BUNKIE Wayfair: lamps, rug, bed frame, **wayfair.ca** | Sarah Richardson Design: headboard, stools, desk chair, sheet set, duvet cover set, throw blanket, **sarahrichardsondesign.com** | Sarah Richardson for Kravet: desk chair fabric, **sarahrichardsondesign.com** | Kravet: accent pillow fabric, headboard, side chair cushion, **kravet.com** | Schumacher: stool fabric, **fschumacher.com** | Miller Island Company: side chair, **millerislandcompany.com** | Dulux: nightstand paint, Blue Beads (DLX160-5), **dulux.ca** | Benjamin Moore: wall paint, Gray Owl (OC-52), **benjaminmoore.ca**.

"FRENCH ACCENT," pages 94 to 105
ENTRYWAY Par Le Trou de la Serrure: hardware, **parletrou.ca** | Alice Tacheny: leather hook, **alicetacheny.com** | Kravet: Mulberry bench cushion fabric, **kravet.com** | Les Ensembliers Design: built-ins, **ensembliers.com**.

DINING ROOM Ralph Lauren: chandelier, **ralphlauren.com** | Le Vestibule: table, **boutiquevestibule.com** | Robert Allen: bench fabric, **robertallendesign.com** | Kravet: Mulberry chair fabric, **kravet.com**.

KITCHEN Lambert & Fils: ceiling fixtures, **lambertetfils.com** | Les Ensembliers Design: built-ins, butcher-block cart, **ensembliers.com** | Par Le Trou de la Serrure: hardware, **parletrou.ca**.

LIVING ROOM Galerie Simon Blais: art, **galeriesimonblais.com** | Kravet: Ralph Lauren sofa fabric, ottoman fabric, wing chair fabric, curtain fabric, Mulberry foot stool fabric, **kravet.com** | Robert Allen: settee fabric, **robertallendesign.com** | Tapis H. Lalonde & Frère: carpet, **tapislalonde.com** | Celadon Collection: table lamps, **celadoncollection.com** | Schumacher: Crescendo armchair fabric, **fschumacher.com**.

BATHROOM Beige Furniture: round mirror, **beigestyle.com** | Forges Urbaines: wall sconce, **forgesurbaines.com** | Chintz & Company: Hazelton House fabric, **chintz.com** | Les Ensembliers Design: built-in, **ensembliers.com**.

LOFT LOUNGE Par Le Trou de la Serrure: hardware, **parletrou.ca** | Red Carpet & Rugs: carpet, **theredcarpet.ca** | Galerie Simon Blais: art, **galeriesimonblais.com**.

BEDROOM Theo: Holland & Sherry bed fabric, **theodecor.com** | Beige Furniture: nightstand, **beigestyle.com** | Loro Piana: Crescendo blanket fabric, **us.loropiana.com** | Red Carpet & Rugs: carpet, **theredcarpet.ca**.

"NOUVEAU VICTORIAN," pages 106 to 121
KITCHEN Wayfair: pendants, sconces, barstools, bar fridge, stand mixer, accent pillows, ottoman, side table, **wayfair.ca** | Kravet: roman blind fabric, **kravet.com** |

New Age Granite: marble backsplash, **newagegranite.com** | Caesarstone: kitchen counter, **caesarstone.ca** | Dinuovo Granite & Marble Inc.: countertop and backsplash fabrication, **905-660-9910** | Taps Bath: Blanco sinks and faucets, **tapsbath.com** | Monogram: fridge, stove, hood vent with custom cladding, **monogram.ca** | Fiber & Cloth: flooring, **fiberandcloth.com** | Sarah Richardson Design: lounge chairs, **sarahrichardsondesign.com** | CB2: cabinet knobs, **cb2.com** | Eclectisaurus: hand sculptures, candlesticks, **eclectisaurus.com** | Glidden: cabinetry paint, Lakefront Blue (90BG 31/124), **glidden.com**.

DINING ROOM Wayfair: rug, dining table, dining chairs, console, blue dinnerware, lanterns, walnut block end table, cement candles, faceted candles, vase, plant basket, **wayfair.ca** | Herman Miller: George Nelson Bubble Lamp, **hermanmiller.com** | Fiber & Cloth: flooring, **fiberandcloth.com** | Kravet: drapery, roman blind fabric, **kravet.com** | Sarah Richardson Design: wallpaper, **sarahrichardsondesign.com** | Toronto Image Works: image printing, **torontoimageworks.com** | Victor Gallery Frames: frames for gallery wall, **victorgallery.ca** | Canadian Drapery Hardware: drapery hardware, **cdhltd.com**.

MUDROOM Wayfair : round mirror with shelf, basket, **wayfair.ca** | Saltillo Tiles: floor tiles, **saltillo-tiles.com** | Metrie: closet doors, **metrie.com** | Caesarstone: stairwell trim, **caesarstone.ca**.

LIVING ROOM Wayfair: rug, pendants, chairs, side tables, lamps, ottoman, ceiling sconces, credenza, black wicker stool, task lamp, **wayfair.ca** | Permanent Press Editions: art prints, **permanentpresseditions.com** | Enviro: gas fireplace, Q3 model, **enviro.com** | New Age Granite & Marble: fireplace marble, **newagegranite.com** | Dinuovo Granite & Marble Inc.: fireplace fabrication, **905-660-9910** | EQ3: sofa, mirrors, black bowl, **eq3.com** | Smash Salvage: constellations art print, **smashsalvage.com** | Elgin Picture & Frame: framing, **elginpictureandframe.com** | Tonic Living: accent pillows, **tonicliving.ca** | Ikea: cabinetry for benches, crib mattresses for cushion topper, **ikea.com** | Premier Prints: drapery fabric, **premierprintsinc.com**.

GREEN BEDROOM Wayfair: pendant, mirrors, stool, baskets, task lamps, bed frames, bedding, boxes, pillow, accessories, **wayfair.ca** | Sarah Richardson for A Street Prints by Brewster: wallpaper, **sarahrichardsondesign.com** | Premier Prints: accent pillow fabric, **premierprintsinc.com** | Kravet: accent pillow fabric, **kravet.com** | Dulux: nightstand paint, Autumn Crisp (70GY 30/254), **dulux.ca**.

ORANGE BEDROOM Wayfair: rug, pendant, side table, bed frame, bench, bedding, basket, **wayfair.ca** | Sarah Richardson for

A Street Prints by Brewster: wallpaper, **sarahrichardsondesign.com** | Bungalow 5: side tables, **bungalow5.com** | Eclectisaurus: lamps, **eclectisaurus.com** | Tonic Living: Roman blind, pillow fabrics, **tonicliving.com** | EQ3: floor lamp, **eq3.com**.

BATHROOM Wayfair: mirrors, sconces, pendant light, towel bar, **wayfair.ca** | Saltillo Tiles: floor tiles, shower tiles, backsplash, **saltillo-tiles.com** | The Rubinet Faucet Company: all plumbing fixtures, **rubinet.com** | Taps Bath: tub, sinks, **tapsbath.com** | Adanac Glass: shower glass, **adanacglass.com** | Ikea: vanity, hardware, **ikea.com** | Dinuovo Granite & Marble Inc.: counter fabrication, **905-660-9910** | Glidden: paint, Swiss White (30BG 72/017), **glidden.com**.

MEDIA ROOM Wayfair: chairs, rug, bar fridge, basket, sconce, wicker stool, ottomans, velvet pillows, credenza, nook pillows, nook side table, **wayfair.ca** | Sarah Richardson for A Street Prints by Brewster: wallpaper, **sarahrichardsondesign.com** | Adanac Glass: glass stair railing, **adanacglass.com** | Creative Design Stairs & Railings: stairs, **cdsr.ca** | Caesarstone: countertop, **caesarstone.ca** | Dinuovo Granite & Marble Inc.: countertop fabrication, **905-660-9910** | Fiber & Cloth: vinyl flooring, **fiberandcloth.com** | Ikea: bar cabinetry, faucet, sink, **ikea.com** | EQ3: sofa, wood block stools, bowl on bar, **eq3.com** | Eclectisaurus: lamp, **eclectisaurus.com** | Tonic Living: nook pillows, **tonicliving.com** | Kiondo: large wood bowl, hanging wall bowls, **kiondo.com**. | Glidden: paint, Roma Haze Grey (10YY 54/034), **glidden.com**.

LAUNDRY ROOM Wayfair: star baskets, **wayfair.ca** | GE Appliances: washer, dryer, **geappliances.com** | Ikea: Besta cabinetry, butcher-block counter customized into waterfall counter, **ikea.com** | EQ3: round wall hooks, **eq3.com**.

BARN Wayfair: chairs, string lights, pendant, dinnerware, **wayfair.ca** | Smash Salvage: bench, **smashsalvage.com** | Heirloom 142: table runner, enamel pitcher, jugs, **heirloom142.com** | Filter (formerly Queen West Antiques): table bases, **filter.design**.

EXTERIOR AND DECK Wayfair: side tables, chairs, sofa, accent pillows, coffee table, tray, planters, outdoor lighting, **wayfair.ca** | Steel Tile Roofing: metal roofing, **steeltile.com** | Martin Windows: windows, **fenetresmartin .com** | Sentinel Solar: solar panels, **sentinelsolar.com** | Dulux: exterior and deck wall paint, Charcoal Slate, **dulux.ca**.

"COASTAL COLONIAL," pages 122 to 133
KITCHEN Saltillo Imports: wall tiles, **saltillo -tiles.com** | Hanford Cabinet & Woodworking: cabinetry, **hanfordcabinet.com** | The Door

Store: cabinetry hardware, **thedoorstore.ca** | Primavera Interior Furnishings: roman blind fabric, **primavera.ca** | Vaughan Designs: pendants, **vaughandesigns.com**.

SITTING ROOM Residential Lighting Studio: star pendant, **residentiallightingstudio.com** | Bilbrough & Co.: bench upholstery fabric, **bilbroughs.com** | Sarah Richardson Design: sofas, **sarahrichardsondesign.com** | Primavera Interior Furnishings: white table lamp in background, **primavera.ca**.

DINING ROOM The Antique and Artisan Gallery: sideboard, **theantiqueandartisangallery.com** | Sharon O'Dowd Custom Furniture: dining table, **sharonodowd.com** | John Rosselli Antiques: dining chairs, **johnrosselliantiques.com** | Greenwich Living Antiques & Design Centre: armchairs, lantern, **greenwichlivingantique.com** | Saltillo Imports: floor tiles, **saltillo-tiles.com** | Fabric.com: drapery fabric, **fabric.com** | Decorum Decorative Finds: yellow table lamps, **ddfhome.com** | The Antique and Artisan Gallery: elephant side table, **theantiqueandartisangallery.com** | Papiers de Paris: mural, **papiersdeparis.com** | Kravet Canada: armchair upholstery fabric, **kravetcanada.com** | Bilbrough & Co.: drapery trim, **bilbroughs.com**.

DEN Y&Co.: drapery and roman blind fabric, **ycocarpet.com** | Bilbrough & Co.: grasscloth wallpaper by Schumacher, sofa upholstery fabric, **bilbroughs.com** | Sarah Richardson Design: sofa, **sarahrichardsondesign.com** | Vintage Fine Objects: mirror, **vintagefineobjects.com**. | Benjamin Moore: trim colour, Charcoal Slate (HC-178), **benjaminmoore.ca**.

POWDER ROOM Farrow & Ball: wallpaper, **farrow-ball.com** | The Rubinet Faucet Company: faucet, **rubinet.com**.

BLUE BATHROOM Hamptons Antique Galleries: mirror, sconces, **hamptonantique galleries.com** | Restoration Hardware: faucet, **restorationhardware.com**.

PINK BEDROOM Kravet Canada: striped grasscloth, **kravet.com** | Cocoon Furnishings: armchair by Lee Industries, **cocoonfurnishings.ca** | Kravet Canada: bench upholstery fabric, **kravetcanada.com** | Lee Jofa: armchair upholstery fabric, **leejofa.com** | The Antique and Artisan Gallery: side table, **theantiqueandartisangallery.com** | Dash & Albert: rug, **dashandalbert.com**.

BLUE BEDROOM Primavera Interior Furnishings: drapery fabric, **primavera.ca** | Farrow & Ball: wallpaper, **farrow-ball.com** | Lee Jofa: mattress fabric, **leejofa.com** | Cynthia Findlay Antiques: plates, **cynthiafindlay.com**.

Introduction to Virtual Reality

Springer
London
Berlin
Heidelberg
New York
Hong Kong
Milan
Paris
Tokyo

John Vince

Introduction to Virtual Reality

 Springer

John Vince
National Centre for Computing Animation
Bournemouth University, UK

British Library Cataloguing in Publication Data
Vince, John (John A.)
    Introduction to virtual reality
    1. Virtual reality
    I. Title
    006
    ISBN 1852337397

Library of Congress Cataloging-in-Publication Data
Vince, John (John A.)
    Introduction to virtual reality / John Vince.
        p. cm.
    ISBN 1-85233-739-7 (alk. paper)
        1. Human-computer interaction. 2. Virtual reality. 3. Computer graphics. 4.
    Three-dimensional display systems. I. Title.
    QA76.9.H85V525 2004
006.8--dc22   2003065304

ISBN 1-85233-739-7 Springer-Verlag London Berlin Heidelberg
Springer-Verlag is part of Springer Science+Business Media GmbH
springeronline.com

Microsoft, MS, Windows, Windows NT and Windows 95 are trademarks of Microsoft Corporation Ltd; 3BALL, STAR*TRAK, ULTRATRAK, FASTRACK, ISOTRACK and INSIDETRAK are trademarks of Polhemus; CyberGlove is a trademark of Virtual Technologies; PUSH, FS^2, BOOM3C, PINCH are trademarks of Fakespace, Inc; OpenGVS is a trademark of Gemini Technology; RealiMation is a trademark of Datapath Ltd; Cosmo is a trademark of Silicon Graphics, Inc; Render Ware is a trademark of Criterion Ltd; Brender is a trademark of Argonaut Software Ltd; NETIMMERSE is a trademark of Numerical Design; SimStudio is a trademark of Ndimension; Torch is a trademark of Newfire; SurRender is trademark of Hybrid; WorldToolkit is trademark of Sense8; MGL is a trademark of SciTech; SoftVR is a trademark of Soft Reality.

Typesetting Gray Publishing, Tunbridge Wells, England
34/3830-543210 Printed on acid-free paper SPIN 10923658

Contents

1
Virtual Reality

1.1 Introduction

During the last decade the word *virtual* became one of the most exposed words in the English language. Today, we have *virtual* universities, *virtual* offices, *virtual* pets, *virtual* graveyards, *virtual* exhibitions, *virtual* wind tunnels, *virtual* actors, *virtual* studios, *virtual* museums, and *virtual* doctors – and all because of *virtual* reality (VR).

The VR hit the headlines in the mid-1980s, and spawned a series of conferences, exhibitions, television programmes, and philosophical debates about the meaning of reality. And overnight, everything suddenly had a virtual dimension – from shopping to sex!

1.2 What Is VR?

Such public enthusiasm for a new technology was totally unexpected, but was not wasted by the VR industry, who were more than keen to exploit every printed word and televised image about their products. Long queues of inquisitive people would form at VR exhibitions to discover what it would be like to experience an immersive computer-generated world. Five minutes though, was more than enough to convince the would-be cyber-citizen that the reality of VR was mostly virtual. The virtual worlds were not as enthralling as had been promised, and something called 'lag' meant that the displayed images were not always in synch with head movements. Although there was some disappointment with these embryonic systems, it was clear that, with time, the technology had an exciting future. Today, VR has evolved into a variety of configurations based upon head-mounted displays (HMDs), personal computers (PCs), workstations, cave automation virtual environments (CAVEs), large screen systems, and virtual tables.

1

Early VR systems described a computer technology that enabled a user to look through a special display called an HMD – and instead of seeing the normal world, they saw a computer-generated world. One of the perceived advantages of this approach was the way it integrated the user with the virtual images. To begin with, the user's head movements are monitored electronically and fed back to the computer creating the images, so that as the user moves their head, objects in the scene remain stationary – just as they do in real life. Most HMDs prevent the wearer from seeing the real world, which, together with a stereoscopic view, quickly immerses them in the substitute world.

There is a natural temptation to reach out and touch virtual objects, even though they do not exist. And this is where VR offers something new – it does allow the user to reach out and move objects about, as if they existed. Just how this is achieved will be described later, but for now, let us assume that it is possible.

If it were possible to build a system that enabled a user to move about a virtual world and interact with it, then it would have extraordinary applications. It would be possible to go on virtual holidays, test drive virtual cars, and even interact with virtual actors in three-dimensional (3D) television. Car designers could design concept cars and explore them at a virtual level long before they were built. Surgeons could practice operations on virtual cadavers, and master delicate manoeuvres before performing a real operation. The applications are limitless – but it all hinges on whether it is possible to build such systems, and what our expectations are.

But VR is much more than immersive systems working with an HMD, and we will discuss such systems throughout this book.

1.3 Who Should Read This Book?

As soon as VR became established as a major area of study, a number of books surfaced on the subject covering everything from how to build a VR system in your garage, to what the virtual world would be like in the year 2050. As VR matured, further books appeared addressing hardware and software issues, and the research effort that would be needed to make VR really happen.

Today, VR is moving very quickly and there is an ever-increasing population wanting to know more about this exciting subject, but do not necessarily want to know too much about the underlying mathematical techniques. If you fall into this category, then this book is for you.

1.4 The Aims and Objectives of This Book

The aim of this book is to take the lid off VR and describe exactly what it is about – and I will attempt to achieve this without using any mathematical notation. There are other excellent books that address this aspect of VR.

My objectives are many. After reading this book:

- you should be able to understand the principles behind a typical VR system;
- you should be able to develop some of these principles into the design of new VR systems;
- you will understand the jargon used within VR; and
- you will be able to communicate to VR specialists any personal requirements you may have for your own VR system.

No doubt, there will be some readers who will want to delve deeper into the mathematics, 3D geometry, and the software used in VR, and this book will provide that first step towards this exciting subject.

1.5 Assumptions Made in This Book

I have not made very many assumptions about you, the reader. Basically, I assume that you understand what a computer is and how it works. You, probably, already know that computers can be used to create images. Perhaps you have already seen such images in recent films such as *Perfect Storm* containing amazing computer-generated special effects. You may even have experienced a VR system, or seen television programmes about VR. But also I am hoping that you are eager to learn more about how the technology works and how it is being applied.

1.6 How to Use This Book

This book has been designed to be read from cover to cover. Each chapter covers concepts and techniques that are developed in subsequent chapters. But obviously where the reader feels that they already are familiar with the subject of a chapter, then simply jump ahead.

1.7 Some VR Concepts and Terms

A typical dictionary definition of the word *virtual* is *being something in effect but not in actual name or form* – and the words *virtual reality* conjure up a vision of a reality without requiring the physical nuts and bolts, or whatever else is needed to build that reality. However, the use of the word *virtual* in *virtual reality* came about because of the *virtual* images generated by the HMD systems. For example, when you look in a mirror and see a reflection of yourself, the image is called a *virtual image*. Even though the reflection appears very realistic, there is no way you can touch it – hence its name.

Now the term *virtual image* was invented long before computers were ever invented, and has been borrowed by the VR community to describe the phenomenon of looking at images that appear to exist.

What we refer to as *reality* is based upon something we call the *external physical world*. This universe – whatever it is – can only be explored by our senses, and we learn from an early age to describe our experiences in terms of colour, sound, temperature, smell, taste, touch, etc. Therefore, a VR seems to suggest a reality that is believable, and yet does not physically exist. But what do we mean by *believable*? Well, *believe* means *to accept as real or true*. But for how long could we be deceived by an alternate reality? One second? One minute? One hour? Furthermore, what do we mean by *true*?

Immediately one senses this pedantic approach to defining the words *virtual reality* is leading us nowhere fast. This, too, became very evident to followers of VR in the early days of the technology. And it soon became apparent, that computers could not, at the time, create virtual worlds that were as believable as the real world. Nor can they today, although some systems are coming close.

During the 1990s, the terms *virtual environments* (VEs) and *synthetic environments* emerged. And although the term VR has persisted – for it always grabs the headlines – there is a general acceptance that VR is about creating acceptable substitutes for real objects or environments, and is *not* really about constructing imaginary worlds that are indistinguishable from the real world.

1.8 Navigation and Interaction

Basically, VR is about using computers to create images of 3D scenes with which one can navigate and interact. By the term navigate, we imply the ability to move around and explore the features of a 3D scene such as a building; while interact implies the ability to select and move objects in a scene, such as a chair.

In order to navigate and interact we require real-time graphics, which implies fast computers. Navigating and interacting with the real world have certain advantages if we are equipped with stereoscopic sight; and the same advantages are realized, if our computer-generated images are also stereoscopic. Naturally, such a demand puts an even higher requirement on a computer's processing capability.

1.9 Immersion and Presence

In 1965 Ivan Sutherland published a paper 'The ultimate display' (Sutherland, 1965) that described how one day, the computer would provide a window into virtual worlds. In 1968 he built an HMD that presented to the user left and right views of a computer-generated 3D scene, such that when the user's head is moved, the virtual scene remained stationary. The images were far from life like – they were simple line drawings. But as they were stereoscopic the user perceived an impression of looking at a solid 3D object. VR was born.

Unfortunately, the 1960s and 1970s was not a period renowned for low-cost, fast computers and consequently VR remained dormant. In the 1980s real-time computer graphics became a reality, and VR became a commercial reality. Initially, early VR systems comprised a real-time computer system, an HMD, and an interactive glove. Apart from supplying the user with stereoscopic images, the HMD immersed the user in the virtual world by preventing them from seeing the real world. Immersion increased the sensation of presence within the virtual world, and for some people, immersion distinguished VR systems from other types of real-time computer graphics systems. For this community, a VR system had to provide a user with a 'first-person' view of the virtual world. Looking at a workstation screen was not VR – it was just fast computer graphics!

1.9.1 Immersive and Non-immersive VR

During the 1990s everyone relaxed their earlier rigid views about what comprised a VR system, and accepted a wider definition for VR. Computer systems emerged capable of displaying real-time images of 3D environments that could be navigated and support interaction, and also they could be configured to support an HMD. Obviously, they were a VR system – but not as powerful as their more expensive partners.

The technology of HMDs has taken much longer to perfect than many people had anticipated. There has also been some resistance to using HMDs over long periods of time. They can be tiring, and some people just do not like the sensation of being visually isolated from their surroundings. This has meant that in some applications, the advantages of VR have had to be appreciated using a mix of immersive and non-immersive techniques. Virtual prototyping using computer-aided design (CAD) is one such application.

Now this has caused many to rethink just, What is VR? Does a VR system have to have an HMD? Can a VR system be nothing more than a PC fitted with an appropriate graphics board? Or can VR be any computer-based system that supports the navigation and interaction with a 3D environment? In an attempt to answer these questions it may be useful to consider those techniques that should not be considered as VR.

1.10 What Is Not VR?

Ever since it was realized that computers could be used to create images, the subject of computer graphics has evolved further and been applied to almost every aspect of graphic design. Today, computer-generated graphics are found in desktop publishing systems, data visualization systems, computer games, television programmes, flight simulators, and behind some of the most amazing special effects in films. But are they all VR? Well this question is open to dispute.

Take, for example, computer games. Although the first computer games operated in real time, the graphics were two-dimensional (2D), and in no way could be considered as VR. Today, many computer games are 3D and provide an incredible variety of scenarios. One can fly fighter planes over realistic terrain; drive sports cars around recognizable grand prix circuits; and test one's skills as a special agent fighting a similar foreign agent. Just take a look at the recent *Grand Theft Auto: Vice City*.

Such games definitely employ the elements of 3D navigation and interaction, and I am quite happy to embrace them as VR systems. Computer games technology is evolving very fast, and games systems will probably become a major sector of VR.

But what about film special effects? Today, most films contain some form of computer-generated special effects, but they cannot be considered as VR. To begin with, the actors are not aware of the virtual characters, such as dinosaurs, passengers on the *Titanic*, or alien creatures. Actors are directed to look towards where a synthetic character is supposed to be, and act appropriately. Then at the post-production stage, the live action is integrated with the computer-generated elements to produce the final film. At no time during the making of the film do the actors see their virtual cast or VEs. They are unable to navigate virtual worlds, and cannot undertake any form of interaction.

Film special effects companies have produced some truly amazing computer-generated scenarios, but they are not VR – they are excellent examples of computer animation, which is another subject!

For example, the image shown in Plate 9 is computer generated and depicts a boat floating on an undulating sea. Although the artist determined the colours of the boat and the sea, the reflections of the boat in the sea were automatically computerized by the software. Even though everything is virtual, there is no computer available today capable of running the rendering software in real time. If we assume that this image took approximately 10 min to render on a workstation, we could produce six images an hour. But in a VR system we require something in the order of 20 per second! Which means that there is a speed factor of 12,000 between the two systems. Therefore, we will have to wait some time before it is possible to simulate such scenarios in real time.

1.11 The Internet

In recent years, the Internet has become established and is transforming the way governments govern, companies trade, and even the way ordinary individuals interact with one another. Although the Internet was used initially to communicate text and 2D graphics, it was soon realized that it could be used to process 3D computer graphics. Almost overnight virtual reality modelling language (VRML) appeared and enabled Internet browsers to interact with 3D environments.

VRML is a language for modelling objects and environments using very simple commands, which can be downloaded as a VRML file over the Internet. With the aid of a suitable browser, the VRML descriptions are interpreted locally to create an image. Special instructions are available to support animation interaction and navigation, which, as we have seen, are the general features of a VR system.

Although VRML models and environments are simple, there is no reason why they should not eventually be able to support very sophisticated designs. However, while we wait for these developments, the Internet is perceived to be a powerful medium for VR. And there is every chance it will develop into a major sector for future VR work.

We will take a look at VRML in Chapter 6 to learn a little about the language syntax, examples of models and potential applications.

1.12 Summary

In this chapter I have attempted to give a brief overview of what VR is about, and we have seen that navigation, interaction, immersion and presence are characteristics of VR systems. The term VR is also mistakenly being associated with processes that are definitely not VR, especially in the field of special effects in films. Basically, a VR system uses real-time computer graphics in such a way to make the user believe that they are part of a virtual domain. This can be achieved using an HMD, hand-held BOOM display, a CAVE, virtual table, dome or a panoramic screen system. But not everyone has access to such technology and PCs, and workstations play a major role in screen-based VR systems.

In the end however, it is not up to me or anyone else to dictate what VR should or should not be. We must be prepared to accept that VR technology will undergo dramatic developments during the next few years, and what we currently accept as VR could disappear and be replaced by something equally revolutionary. For the moment though, I will continue with the above definition and proceed to explore the essential elements of VR.

2

The Benefits of VR

2.1 Introduction

Although we live in an age where we can buy things that serve no purpose what so ever, most products have to provide a service and offer real benefits. In industry, it would be unthinkable to employ any technique or technology that did not add value in some form or another. For example, once upon a time, computers were more trouble than they were worth. They were unreliable, software was problematical, and if one could get by without using them, then that was the preferred course of action.

Today, it would be unthinkable for any company not to consider using computers. Even though computers will 'crash' occasionally, and software collapses regularly, their advantages are enormous. And as industry embraces the Internet and adjusts to the concept of global markets, the age of digital communication is here to stay. But when a revolutionary technology such as virtual reality (VR) comes along, it is only natural that industry reacts with caution.

A first and natural reaction was to ask searching questions about cost, performance, life cycles, upgrades, training, software availability, benefits, etc. Unfortunately, 15 years ago when VR systems were just emerging, the answers to these questions were vague and not very inspiring. VR companies were hoping that some industrial sectors would share their own vision of VR, and take a similar gamble. Failure would not destroy the company, but success promised real rewards.

Fortunately, some companies did accept the challenge of VR. And as one might have expected, some projects failed, but others prospered, and today, such projects have identified clear and viable markets for VR.

My personal opinion at the time was that it would be unthinkable for any company to suddenly embrace a new technology and adopt new and unproved methods and procedures. VR was so revolutionary that the only way for it to be accepted was that

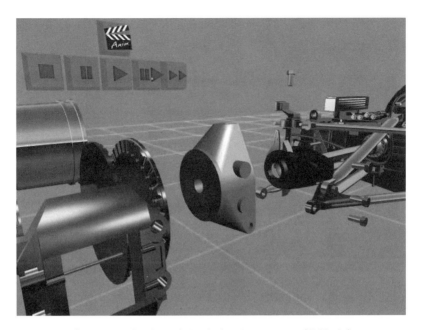

Figure 2.1 Exploded view of a CAD database. Image courtesy of Division Ltd.

it should complement rather than replace any existing process. For example, one special application for VR is in the computer-aided design (CAD) industry, where three-dimensional (3D) components and assemblies are already being designed at a virtual level. VR could not have replaced the workstation approach to CAD. To begin with, the software was not available, nor could the systems handle large CAD databases. However, what VR could do was to provide a valuable simulation and visualization environment for evaluating CAD models. Today, this is developing into a prosperous sector for VR. Figure 2.1 shows an exploded view of an assembly that can be viewed in real time from any point of view. By activating the virtual video cassette recorder (VCR) controls the individual components move to show how the assembly is constructed.

2.2 3D Visualization

We have all become accustomed to working with computers using monitors or liquid crystal display (LCD) screens. They have been with us for so long that it is hard to imagine any other way or working without computers. But it is equally hard to imagine that we will be using screens 50 or 100 years from now. There has to be new technological developments that will completely transform this user interface.

For the moment, though, traditional computer graphic systems display images of 3D scenes upon the flat screen of a monitor. Even though the scenes may be very realistic, we are aware that we are looking at a two-dimensional (2D) image, when perhaps we should be looking at a 3D scene. It is still a question of us, the viewer, looking at the computer holding the image.

Immersive VR transforms all of these by making the user part of the virtual environment (VE). A head-mounted display (HMD) or cave automation virtual environment (CAVE) provides the wearer with a 'first-person' view of the virtual scene and effectively places the user next to, or inside the virtual object. We know from experience the value of seeing and touching something, rather than looking at a photograph.

A photograph of a car may be very accurate and realistic, but nothing can replace the sense of scale, proportion, colour, and visual impact of being next to a real car. Simply by walking around a car we can take in subtle changes in its surface geometry. We notice how highlights travel along body panels, and how concave features are blended with convex features. We notice the relationship of the interior to the exterior, and how one blends into the other. Just imagine what it would be like to explore the ray-traced images shown in Plates 1 and 2 in real time. Currently, this is impossible, but one day it will happen.

There are myriad reasons why a flat image is inferior to a 3D view of a solid object, which is why VR offers so much to 3D visualization. The key question, however, is what value does one place upon being able to explore a virtual interior design in 3D as shown in Fig. 2.2, rather than 2D?

Figure 2.2 A visualization of an interior design created by the LightWorks rendering system. Image courtesy of LightWorks Design.

If designers can get by without using HMDs and VR, then so be it. But the same could have been said about replacing traditional engineering drawing with CAD systems. Yes, it was possible to get by without CAD, but it was also impossible to progress without CAD. The CAD systems have transformed the way we design digital processors, cars, planes, rockets, satellites, offshore platforms, etc.; and many of these structures would have been impossible to build without the help of computers. Even the humble washing machine exists in a virtual form long before a physical model is constructed (Plate 3).

We could not have landed on the moon without computers and CAD. And as we prepare to colonize planets within our solar system, CAD models such as the one shown in Fig. 2.3 are being used to visualize future space missions and the construction of space cities.

CAD also plays a vital role in the design of chemical plants whose complexity defies the imagination (Fig. 2.4). Such structures would be impossible to build without computers and today's sophisticated software tools. And as this complexity increases, we will require even more sophisticated tools for visualizing these structures.

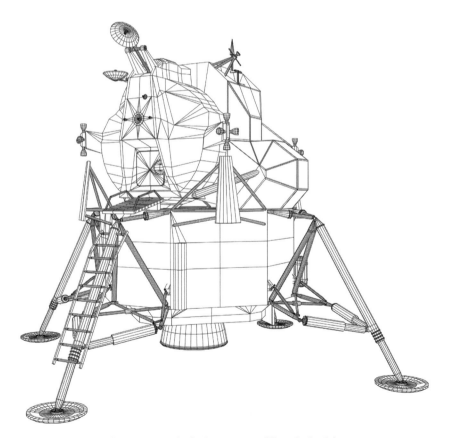

Figure 2.3　Moon lander. Image courtesy of Viewpoint DataLabs.

Figure 2.4   External and internal visualization of a chemical plant. Images courtesy of Virtual Presence.

On a much smaller scale, take for example, the problem of designing a car wheel (Fig. 2.5). Prior to the days of CAD, it would have taken an experienced draftsperson many hours of work creating detailed orthographic projections of the curved features. Today, with the benefit of CAD, it can be designed in a fraction of time, and also visualized as a 3D object. But VR takes us one step further; with VR it is possible to see a set of wheels attached to a virtual car, and inspect the car from any point of view in real time.

It is highly likely that today's CAD systems will become tomorrow's VR systems. And already one can see how the benefits of visualization offered by VR are being integrated into the CAD methodology. However, this does not imply that future CAD designers will be wearing HMDs. They may still translate their ideas into concepts using screens of some sort, but they will also rely upon projection systems, as well as HMDs to view their designs.

Figure 2.5   A car wheel modelled on a PC using Lightwave. Image courtesy of James Hans.

Another thing to bear in mind is that where VR attempts to make the user part of the virtual domain, other 3D technologies are under development that make 3D virtual objects part of the real world. For example, 3D television sets already exist in research laboratories, and other forms of 3D computer displays are being developed. And it is highly likely that in the near future it will be possible to display realistic views of virtual objects that can be manipulated directly by our hands and fingers.

2.3 Navigation

2.3.1 Immersive VR

It was mentioned in Chapter 1 that navigation and interaction are important features of a VR system. In immersive VR, navigation is made possible by tracking the position of the user's head in three dimensions, such that when they move forward, they pass by objects that are no longer in front of them. And when they turn their head, they see those objects that were beyond their field of view (FOV). We take such phenomena for granted in the real world – it just happens naturally.

However, there is a problem if the user wishes to walk about the virtual world, especially if it is rather large. To begin with, a cable connects the user's HMD to the computer, which may only extend a few metres. Secondly, the head-tracking technology that may only operate over a short radius of a few metres also restricts the user's mobility. But all is not lost. It is possible to navigate a VE without physically moving. All that is necessary is to instruct the host computer to 'fly' towards a certain direction, as instructed by the user. Such instructions are communicated via a hand-held 3D mouse. The direction is often determined by the user's gaze direction. For example, if the user is looking along a virtual corridor, simply by pressing a mouse button, the user will apparently drift along the corridor until giving a 'stop' instruction. By gazing in another direction and issuing the 'fly' command, the user can navigate the maze of corridors without his or her feet ever leaving the ground.

Similar instructions can be used to ascend and descend flights of stairs. Which means that it is possible to move about virtual houses, submarines, oil platforms, cities, offices, chemical refineries, nuclear power stations, and any other structure stored in the computer. Effective though this may be, it does create problems for those people who are sensitive to motion sickness – but more of this later.

2.3.2 Desktop VR

So far we have only looked at navigation using immersive VR. Non-immersive or desktop VR systems must be navigated using totally different techniques.

Somehow we need to communicate to the host software how we wish to move in 3D space. For example, we may wish to go forward, backward, left, right, up, or down. But we may also require to stand still and rotate left or right, or look up or down. Now in an immersive system this can be achieved through head movements, but without a 3D tracker other hardware or special interface tools are required.

One solution is to use a joystick or a 3D mouse as shown in Fig. 2.6. These devices can communicate three directions of translation and rotations about three axes. But without such useful physical devices we must resort to some virtual subterfuge. An approach that has been successful with Internet browsers is to use two or three screen controls that work in conjunction with a conventional 2D mouse. Figure 2.7 shows a control panel where the button on the left controls the translating movements left, right, up, and down; the centre button controls moving forwards, backwards, turning left and right; and the button on the right is responsible for tilting downwards and upwards. Simply by clicking on one of these buttons and moving the mouse in an appropriate direction one can navigate with ease through complex 3D VEs.

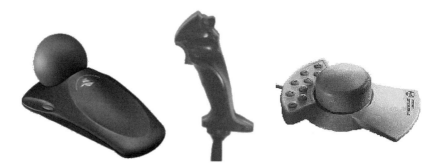

Figure 2.6 Spaceball by Spacetec. Spacestick by Virtual Presence. Spacemouse by Logitech. Images courtesy of Spacetec, Virtual Presence, and Logitech.

Figure 2.7 The 3D Webmaster's navigation controls.

Figure 2.8   Visualization of a proposed industrial development. Image courtesy of the VR Centre at Teesside University.

To be able to navigate without physically moving opens up an extraordinary range of applications for VR. It implies that one could explore an architect's plans for a house and visualize what would be seen from different rooms. A trainee marine could learn about the interior of a submarine using a VR system, so that when he or she arrived at the real submarine, they would be familiar with different compartments and their access points, and how to operate relevant controls. Personnel expecting to be transferred to an oil platform could learn about the site's emergency procedures using a VR system before being posted. It would be possible to become familiar with foreign cities, new office structures, and chemical refineries, long before they were ever built.

For example, Fig. 2.8 shows an image from a visualization project undertaken by the VR Centre at Teesside University. The aerial view shows very clearly how the proposed development integrates with the green-belt site. But a VR system would allow the project designers to explore the development at ground level and evaluate all sorts of issues and correct them before any concrete had been mixed.

2.4 Interaction

Initially the idea of interacting with virtual objects seems impossible. But it is something we take for granted when working with a word processor. For example, in writing this book, I have been continually cutting text and moving it to a different place. 'Cut and paste' is a technique used extensively throughout software packages.

It saves incredible amounts of time and makes computers just a little more user-friendly.

If we can cut and paste in 2D, it should be possible to perform the same operation in 3D. In 2D we use a mouse to mark the text to be cut, and the cursor position to mark the place to paste. We require a similar process in 3D to identify the object we wish to cut, together with its new position.

2.4.1 Immersive VR

One of the first devices to aid interaction was the interactive glove. When worn by the user its position in space and finger positions are relayed to the host computer. These signals are used to control the position of a virtual hand, and the orientation of its virtual fingers, which the user sees in his or her HMD. Thus as they move their real hand about in space they see the virtual hand duplicate the same movements – delayed slightly by a fraction of second.

Meanwhile, inside the host computer, the geometry of the virtual hand is adjusting to the position of the user's real hand. And as this geometry is defined numerically (more about this later), it can be compared by the host software to see if any of the hand's features collide with the geometry describing the VE, which also has a numerical basis. Fortunately, modern computers can perform these numerical comparisons with great speed, and may only require a few thousandths of a second to undertake this task on a small database. When a collision or interference is detected between the virtual hand and a virtual object, the host software could react by colouring the object red, for example.

The user will see this change in colour as confirmation that a collision has been recognized. The host computer now requires a separate signal to confirm that the selected object is to be moved. On receiving this signal, the virtual object is effectively joined to the user's virtual hand. And wherever the user moves his or her real hand, the object moves with it. When a new place is identified for the object – which can be anywhere, even hanging in space – another signal is given to release it from the user's grasp. Figure 2.9 illustrates the CyberGlove manufactured by Virtual Technologies. It employs two or three bend sensors on each finger, and other sensors to monitor thumb crossover, palm arch, wrist flexion and wrist abduction (bending away from the central axis).

2.4.2 Desktop VR

Interacting with virtual objects on a desktop system is slightly different, but equally easy and effective. For example, it would be possible to position the screen cursor over the required object and by activating a mouse button, the system responds by displaying the object's boundary box. Then, by pressing another mouse button, the object could be dragged to a new position. The top image in Fig. 2.10 shows a greenhouse that has been selected, and the image below shows how the greenhouse has been dragged to a new position using the mouse.

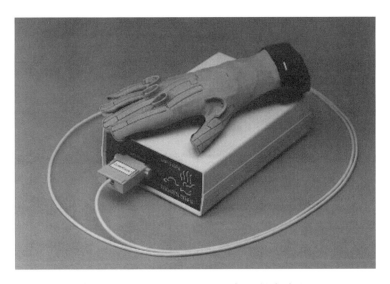

Figure 2.9   CyberGlove. Image courtesy of Virtual Technologies.

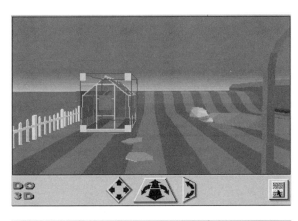

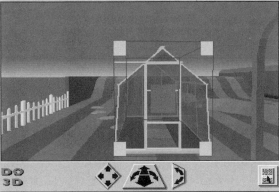

Figure 2.10   Object selection and translation using a conventional mouse.

The ramifications of interacting with VEs are enormous, for it implies that one can interact with and modify the status of any VE. As a trivial example, one could play immersive chess; walking around the board picking up the chess pieces, and then waiting for the computer's response. What such an exercise would achieve is questionable, but the principle is sound. On a higher note, one could experiment with assembling a collection of virtual engineering components to ensure they could be fitted together correctly. And perhaps in an architectural application, an architect could interactively position walls, doors and windows to explore optimum layouts.

The examples are endless and support the concept of undertaking anything from servicing an airplane engine to the intricacies of virtual surgery. We will explore more of these applications later on.

2.5 Physical Simulation

I have mentioned that the user's hand and the database for the VE have a numerical basis, which will be explained in detail in the next chapter. But if numbers are the basis of the VE, one cannot expect virtual objects to mimic accurately his or her physical counterparts. For instance, in the real world when I drop a glass on a hard floor, the glass breaks into an unpredictable number of pieces. It would be too much to expect a virtual glass to behave in the same way if it were dropped. In fact, a virtual glass would not drop if it were let go. It would remain in the position it was released. Virtual objects require virtual gravity, if they are to be subject to an accelerated fall!

But if we implement virtual gravity, what happens when the virtual glass collides with the virtual floor? Nothing – it simply passes through the floor and falls through the virtual world. It only stops falling when the VR software is re-initialized. However, if we want the glass to recognize the floor as a solid object, and explode into a thousand pieces, which in turn fall to the floor, we have a problem. Such exercises require sophisticated simulation software to subject virtual objects to physical forces. It can be done – but not in real time, and therefore not within modern VR systems.

Expecting a VR system to simulate an exploding glass is asking too much of today's technology, but other physical behaviours could be simulated. For example, a ball could be dropped and allowed to bounce. A chair on wheels could be pushed against a wall and a simulated bounce created. A dress could collide with a virtual mannequin's legs as she walked into a room. A piece of virtual flesh could be pulled to explore its elastic properties. It could also be cut into two to mimic a surgical manoeuvre.

The real problem with simulation is the computational power required to evaluate the mathematical equations describing the physical process. If such digital horsepower can be provided by an appropriate supercomputer, without degrading the performance of the VR system, then it is possible to simulate some very sophisticated behaviours.

If behaviours are required for effect rather than physical accuracy, then it is possible to compute in advance an animated sequence of objects. For example, when our virtual glass hits a virtual floor, an animation sequence can be played showing individual glass fragments twisting and tumbling in space. It will look very realistic, but it will look the same whenever we drop a glass!

Simulation, then, is possible, but we cannot reproduce the level of detail (LOD) that occurs in the real world. We will *never* (a very dangerous word to use) be able to experience a virtual beach where virtual bathers are playing in the virtual sea, splashing with virtual waves, while virtual palm trees swing in a virtual breeze. We will *never* be able to simulate this with the same fidelity of the real world. We could not even approach it. However, it could be simulated if we lowered our expectations.

2.6 VEs

Early flight simulators employed scale models of airports upon which trainee pilots acquired flying skills, and experienced pilots were evaluated every 6 months. The models had many disadvantages. To begin with, they were physically large (typically $50\,m^2$). They required skilled people to build them; they required substantial levels of illumination; they were static, and could not show any moving features, such as ground vehicles; they could not reproduce different weather conditions; and furthermore, an airline would require a separate model for every specific airport.

When a pilot was using the simulator, a small video camera moves over the model and relays back to a screen in front of the pilot what was seen from that position in space. The effect was acceptable, but required a significant amount of physical technology. Today, pilots train in simulators using virtual models of airports. Although they still require skilled modellers to construct the numeric database, the models take up no physical space, for they are stored on a computer disk. They require no illumination, for virtual illumination models are used to simulate different times of the day and year. Features of the VE can be animated, such as cars driving along freeways, ground vehicles moving between terminal buildings, and other aircraft landing and taking off. The VEs are available for every major international airport, and copies only take a few minutes to create. And virtual fog, rain, snow, thunder, and lightning can be introduced at the press of a button.

Figure 2.11 shows an image produced by a real-time image generator (IG) manufactured by Evans & Sutherland. It depicts a countryside scene with undulating terrain, trees, cornfields, and dramatic clouds. What is amazing is that it only takes a few thousandths of a second to produce!

Figure 2.12 shows a Boeing 737-800 flight simulator manufactured by Thomson Training & Simulation. The curved structure at the top houses the panoramic mirror that reflects the computer-generated images into the cockpit, and immerses the pilot and co-pilot inside the VE. As they are unable to see the outside world, they have no external cues to help them understand their orientation. Therefore, the motion platform shown supporting the simulator can be used to lean the simulator back to create the sensation of acceleration, or lean forward to create the sensation of deceleration.

All of the computers, including the IGs, are located away from the simulator to keep the moving mass to a minimum. But even then, the platform still weighs several tonnes, and very powerful hydraulic pumps are required to move it in real time.

Figure 2.11   Real-time, 3D image of terrain. Image courtesy of Evans & Sutherland Computer Corporation, Salt Lake City, Utah, USA.

Architects have always relied upon physical models to provide a realistic impression of the finished project. Such models are very expensive to construct; and once built, offer few advantages. It is impossible to navigate the models internally, although small video cameras are often manoeuvred into small corridors to convey interior views. The obvious next step for architects is to embrace VR technology, together with all of its advantages.

The designers of Chartres cathedral for example, only had access to muscle power and primitive mechanical tools, which is why it took many decades to construct. No doubt they employed elevations, projections, and perhaps crude models; but they were unable to visualize the grandeur of the final building. Today, we can store the cathedral's geometry within a computer (Fig. 2.13) and explore it at a virtual level.

Modern architects now have access to the most sophisticated design aids ever invented, making it possible to construct buildings of great complexity, and build them within very short time spans. Furthermore, modern software is capable of incredible realism making it possible to simulate with great accuracy complex lighting conditions. Figure 2.14 and Plates 4, 13, and 14 show the extraordinary level of photo-realism that is possible using modern ray tracing and radiosity renderers.

Manufacturers of submarines go to extraordinary lengths to ensure that the final submarine can be operated successfully and efficiently. Often a scale model of a submarine is constructed and evaluated using suitably scaled mannequins representing sailors. Obviously this is an expensive process, and as the original data is stored within a CAD system, it seems a natural move to undertake evaluation trials at a virtual level.

Figure 2.12   A Boeing 737-800 full-flight simulator for Lufthansa. Image courtesy of Thomson Training & Simulation.

Figure 2.15 shows a simple external view of an attack submarine constructed from approximately 15,000 polygons. Its interior however, is empty, and requires a separate database description that could easily exceed the external complexity by two or three orders of magnitude.

Designers of aero-engines also build physical mock-ups of their latest designs to ensure that it is physically possible to build them without design faults, such as intersecting pipes, inaccessible components, etc. Again, such mock-ups are very expensive to construct, and as the original design is stored within a CAD system, it seems natural to evaluate the physical requirements of the engine at a virtual level.

The benefits of VEs over physical environments are obvious:

- no space is required;
- they can be very accurate and realistic;

Figure 2.13   Chartres cathedral. Image courtesy of Viewpoint DataLabs.

- they can be animated;
- they can be illuminated;
- they can be copied;
- they can be shared;
- they can be navigated; and
- one can interact with them.

What more could one want?

Figure 2.14 Radiosity view of an interior using the LightWorks rendering system. Image courtesy of LightWorks Design.

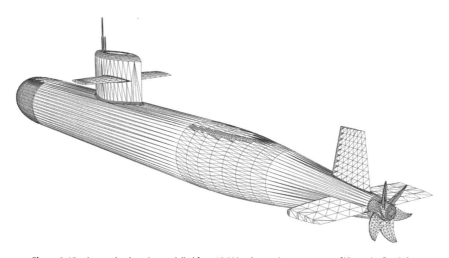

Figure 2.15 An attack submarine modelled from 15,000 polygons. Image courtesy of Viewpoint DataLabs.

However, in spite of these obvious advantages, they still require building, which takes time and special modelling software tools. But as we have just seen, they can easily be converted from CAD databases, and processed to support the requirements of a VR system.

2.6.1 Libraries

In the early days of computer animation, 3D computer models were often very simple and consisted of logos, words, and primitive geometric forms. But with the advent of 3D digitizers and CAD systems more complex models were employed. It was soon realized that such objects had an intrinsic value, and it was futile exercise to model something when the geometry already existed. Perhaps, the largest database of 3D geometry is currently held by Viewpoint DataLabs International. Their catalogue currently lists over 10,000 3D models covering the sectors of air transport, anatomy, animals, architecture, characters, electronics, geography, ground transport, household, industrial, military, leisure, and space. Everything from a human foot to a Harrier jump-jet is available as a set of polygons or non-uniform rational B-splines (NURBS), which are a useful type of curve. Figure 2.16 shows a detailed model of a human head revealing its polygonal structure. Detail such as hair, eyebrows, eyelashes, and colour must be added separately.

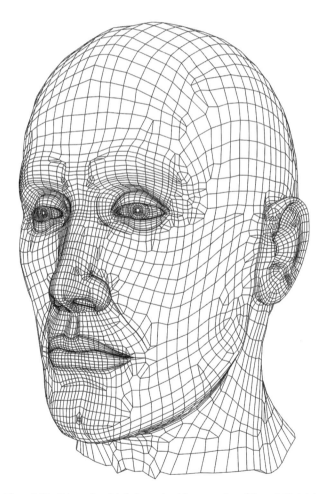

Figure 2.16 Polygonal model of a human head. Image courtesy of Viewpoint DataLabs.

2.7 Applications

Although I do not want to spend too much time at this stage describing various applications for VR, perhaps it is worth exploring the scope and breadth of applications that are potentially possible:

- VR has obvious applications in visualizing structures developed using CAD. The benefits of seeing a product as a true 3D object are immense, and the ability to explore issues of operator visibility, maintenance, manufacture, and physical simulation before anything is built are immeasurable.
- VR has significant benefits in training, especially where it is expensive or dangerous to undertake the training using real systems, such as planes, ships, power stations, oil rigs, etc.
- VR could be used to visualize large building projects where environmental issues are important, and it is important to obtain both exterior and interior views.
- VR could be used in surgical training, where a surgeon can practice surgical procedures on virtual organs, without endangering the lives of real patients.
- VR could be used in totally original ways, such as for virtual television studios, real-time animated characters for children's programmes, and a VE for rehearsing plays.
- VR could be used for building virtual museums, virtual historic buildings, virtual restaurants (Plates 5 and 6), virtual aircraft interiors (Plates 7 and 8), and virtual archaeological sites.
- VR could be used for a million-and-one other applications from art to space exploration.

2.8 Summary

When VR systems first emerged from university research laboratories and were offered to industry as a revolutionary design and visualization tool, it was very difficult to convince industry to embrace the technology. There were confused messages about the applications for VR. Apparently, VR could be used for computer games, keyhole surgery simulators, education and training, engineering design, scientific visualization, the treatment of phobias, and a million-and-one other applications. But there was little evidence of such applications, and those that did exist were not very convincing.

Since these heady days of hype and promise, industry has had an opportunity of putting VR through its paces and helping in its growth. Various industrial sectors have recognized true potential for VR and have worked with VR companies to design systems they can use. Today, it is not difficult to identify the benefits of VR. The examples we have discussed in this chapter are not contrived, nor are they imaginary – they are all happening today.

It has at last been recognized that it takes time to introduce a revolutionary idea. Real commercial benefits must always be identified and quantifiable, and none of this can be rushed. Industry, technology, and commercial climates will dictate the speed with which VR is embraced as an industrial tool.

3

3D Computer Graphics

3.1 Introduction

As you have probably realized, virtual reality (VR) is basically about three-dimensional (3D) computer graphics, and in this chapter we are going to explore some of the techniques used to produce coloured views of virtual environments (VEs).

Computer graphics is an enormous subject, and we only will have time to look at some of the major topics relevant to VR. These include representing 3D VEs, producing a perspective view and colouring the image. Building the VE is called modelling, while image creation is called rendering.

To begin with though, I will put computer graphics in some sort of historical context and show how VR first emerged.

3.2 From Computer Graphics to VR

3.2.1 Computers

In the early 1960s digital computers started to make an impact on commercial organizations and educational institutes. The machines were very large, often requiring air conditioning and several human operators to load punched cards, paper tape, magnetic tapes, and printer paper. Memory size was measured in kilobytes and a 32 kB machine could cost in the order of $100,000.

3.2.2 Graph Plotters

In the early days, the computer's only graphical peripheral was the graph plotter which drew lines on paper using an or ink pen. The size of these devices varied from a dozen inches to several feet, and the drawing speed could vary from a sluggish 3 to 100 cm/s. Some drawings might only take a few minutes but others could easily exceed an hour, and in spite of these display speeds it was soon realized that computers could be used for animation.

To create an animation sequence a program was designed to draw the individual frames upon animation cells that were then back painted and photographed. It was a tedious process, but even then, the computer was seen as a revolutionary creative tool.

3.2.3 Storage Tube Displays

In the 1970s the storage tube transformed computer graphics by providing a high-resolution screen for displaying monochrome (green) line drawings. The major disadvantage of the device was that the only way to erase part of the screen was to erase the entire screen. Thus it was useless for any form of moving image. The screen contents could be output to paper using a special thermal printer.

3.2.4 Video Displays

Video displays exploited the technology of television to use a video signal to produce an image in the form of coloured dots and lines. Video technology however, provided a mechanism for selective erasure, and simple animation.

3.2.5 Frame-Stores

As computer memory became cheaper and more abundant, the frame-store emerged in the mid-1970s. This was capable of storing a single image in the form of a matrix of pixels and opened up the possibility of shaded images. It could still take anything from a few minutes to an hour to create a single image that was output to a videodisk or video recorder.

3.2.6 Rendering

Shading algorithms appeared in the 1970s notably from Gouraud (1971) and Phong (1973), and texture mapping from Blinn and Newell (1976). Other topics such as anti-aliasing, shadows, hidden-surface removal, environment mapping, and modelling strategies kept researchers busy in the USA and the UK.

3.2.7 Real-Time Graphics

Towards the end of the 1970s Ivan Sutherland was experimenting with simple real-time image generators (IGs) that were eventually embraced by the flight simulation industry. By the early 1980s the flight simulator industry became the first to employ VR techniques without realizing it. To them, real-time computer graphics was simulation, and we had to wait a few years for Jaron Larnier to coin the term *virtual reality*.

3.2.8 VR

Since 1965 Ivan Sutherland had realized that computers had an important role to play in real-time graphics, and his early work on head-mounted displays (HMDs) was a constant reminder what the future had in store. However, as with many inventions it can take 10–20 years before an idea is truly realized. Nevertheless, over the past two decades we have witnessed a series of major events that collectively have resulted in today's VR systems. Such events include Cinerama in 1952, Morton Heilig's 'Sensorama' system in 1956, Dan Sandin and Richard Sayre's bend-sensing glove in 1977, the Polhemus tracking system in 1979, and Andy Lippman's interactive videodisk to drive around Aspen in 1980. In 1982, Thomas Zimmerman patented a data glove that used optical sensors, and in 1983, Mark Callahan built a see-through HMD at Massachusetts Institute of Technology (MIT).

During this creative period of invention and discovery various companies pioneered the development of VR hardware and software: notably VPL Research, Inc., W Industries Ltd., Division Ltd., Fakespace, Inc., Polhemus, Virtual Research, Reflection Technologies, Sense 8 Corporation, and Superscape Ltd. Many still exist today, but some, alas, have not managed to survive the intense commercial pressures that pose a constant threat to any embryonic technology.

3.3 Modelling Objects

Computer graphics techniques are employed to visualize a wide variety of things such as graphs, histograms, business graphics, cars, ships, airplanes, dinosaurs, tornadoes, pigs, water, and clouds. To cope with such a wide range of subjects, an equally wide range of tools has evolved to meet the individual requirements of these different structures.

One of the simplest modelling elements used in computer graphics is a flat surface, or polygon. For example, to model a rectangular box, six polygons are required to define its surface (Fig. 3.1). Polygons are ideal for constructing all sorts of regular objects such as bricks, rooms, desks, etc., but are useless for modelling clouds and fog.

To appreciate how a 3D object is stored inside a computer, let us examine a simple example. Figure 3.2 shows an object constructed from four triangles: a base, two

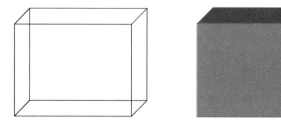

Figure 3.1   Wire frame and shaded view of a six-sided box.

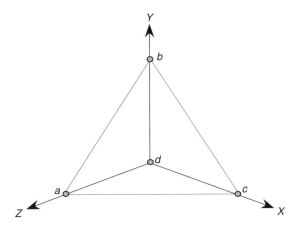

Triangle Table			
Name	**Vertices**		
abc	a	b	c
cbd	c	b	d
adb	a	d	b

Vertex Table			
Name	**x**	**y**	**z**
a	0	0	1
b	0	1	0
c	1	0	0
d	0	0	0

Figure 3.2 Internal storage of a 3D object.

vertical sides, and the side facing us. The vertices (corners) are labelled a, b, c, and d. Each triangle can be identified by its vertices: the side facing us is abc; the base is acd; and the two sides are cbd and adb. Notice that the vertices are defined in a clockwise sequence as seen from a position outside the object.

The object is stored as a *Triangle Table* and a *Vertex Table*. The Triangle Table stores a list of triangles: abc, cbd, and adb, and for each triangle there is a list of vertices. For example, triangle cbd has vertices c, b, and d. With reference to the Vertex Table, vertex c has coordinates $(1, 0, 0)$; b has coordinates $(0, 1, 0)$; and d has coordinates $(0, 0, 0)$. The numbers in brackets are the x, y, and z coordinates, respectively.

The reason for building objects this way is that it is easy to change the geometry of an object. For example, if we wish to move vertex b to a new position, all we have to do is to alter the Vertex Table with a new set of coordinates. The Triangle Table remains unaltered, as the object's underlying geometry has not changed.

Objects such as teapots, telephones, vases, cars, etc. have complex curved surfaces that can be constructed from curved patches. Figure 3.3 shows how the delicate curves of a modern telephone can be modelled from a collection of surface patches. Even the coiled cable can be modelled with great accuracy.

Other objects that must incorporate interior detail, as well as their surface geometry, such as engineering components, are constructed using computer-aided design (CAD) systems, and the techniques are beyond the scope of this text.

Figure 3.3   A virtual telephone modelled from surface patches. Image courtesy of James Hans.

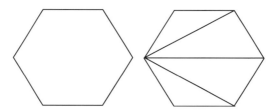

Figure 3.4   A single hexagon and a triangulated hexagon.

Polygons and triangles are very easy to manipulate within a computer and it is possible to create coloured views of them extremely fast. Although other modelling techniques can be used to model objects more accurately, the rendering time, in general, is longer.

We will discover that high-speed rendering is vital to a successful VR system. If there is any delay in producing the images seen by the user, the illusion of immersion and presence are quickly lost. Consequently, the majority of VR systems are built around VEs modelled from polygons or triangles. Between the two, triangles are preferred, as they are consistent, that is they have three sides, and they are always flat. A polygon built from four or more sides can be twisted, which can introduce errors in rendering. Figure 3.4 illustrates how a hexagon would be divided into four triangles.

Objects in the real world are 3D that is, three measurements are required to fix the position of a point in space. Similarly, when describing a polygon for a VE, each

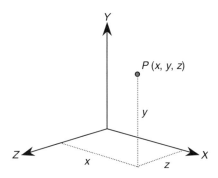

Figure 3.5 A set of Cartesian axes.

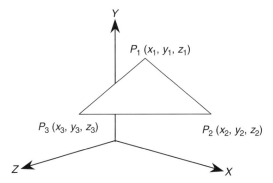

Figure 3.6 A triangle requires nine numbers to encode its three vertices.

vertex (corner) requires three measurements to locate it relative to some reference point called the *origin*. In fact, every polygon in a VE must be described in this way.

Figure 3.5 shows a set of 3D Cartesian axes (90° to each other) labelled X, Y, and Z, intersecting at the origin. These are used to derive the three measurements (coordinates) for each vertex. In this case the point P has coordinates (x, y, z). Figure 3.6 shows a triangle that has three vertices, and requires a total of nine coordinates to fix the vertex positions. More complex objects may require hundreds, thousands, or even hundreds of thousands of coordinates, which can present serious computational problems for the VR host computer. It should not be difficult to appreciate that the number of coordinates is proportional to the complexity of the VE, and the more complex it becomes, the longer it takes to render the image. Consequently, every effort is made to keep the VE as simple as possible.

Special 3D modelling systems are available to construct VEs. Systems such as 3D Studio Max, MultiGen, LightWave, and MAYA are all used to create the coordinate data. When a CAD system has been used, special programs (filters) can be used to convert the CAD data into a polygonal form acceptable to the VR system. For example, McDonnell Douglas has used the Unigraphics II CAD/computer-aided manufacture (CAM) system to model systems such as the F/A-18 tactical strike

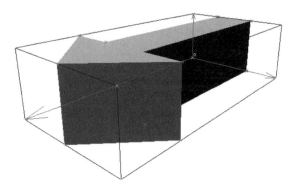

Figure 3.7 A 3D arrow created by extruding an outline.

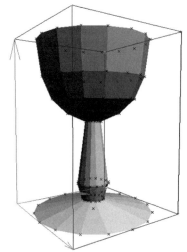

Figure 3.8 A wine glass created by sweeping a contour.

fighter engine, but they have also used Division's dVISE VR software for visualization purposes. To import such CAD databases, filters are generally available for Parametric Technologies, Unigraphics II, CADDS5, Pro/ENGINEER, I-DEAS Master Series, CATIA, and Intergraph Solid Edge.

Certain objects possess different degrees of symmetry. For example, a rectangular box can be imagined as its cross section extruded over its length, and a cylinder can be imagined as a circle extruded over its height. Figure 3.7 shows how a 3D arrow can be created from the shape of an arrow. In order to simplify the construction of such objects inside a computer, special modelling tools are available to aid this process.

Another class of object exhibits symmetry about an axis. For example, the wine glass shown in Fig. 3.8 has a central vertical axis, about which the glass's contour rotates. This and other objects like cups, saucers, teapots, wheels, etc. can be modelled by first designing a simple contour curve, which is then rotated about an axis to develop the

Figure 3.9   Geometric primitives. Courtesy of James Hans.

surface. However, when we draw a curve in the real world it is a smooth continuous line – in a computer it has to be represented as a mathematical equation or a string of straight edges. CAD systems employ mathematical techniques, while VR systems employ simple strings of straight edges. Thus what should appear to be smooth surfaces are often chunky with an obvious faceted structure. No doubt, one day VR systems will be able to handle perfectly smooth objects, but for the moment, models have to be kept as simple as possible.

Extruding and sweeping techniques can be further developed to construct some really complex objects, which saves considerable time when building a VE.

Although 3D modelling systems permit any object to be built from scratch, they also give the user access to a library of pre-built objects. A simple library facility may only provide a variety of boxes, pyramids, spheres, cylinders, cones, etc., but a more advanced facility may give the user access to hundreds of 3D objects, and perhaps entire VEs. Other systems offer an extensive warehouse of objects that include geometric primitives, buildings, lights, people, plants, streets, and toys. Figure 3.9 shows a typical range of geometric primitives.

3.4 Dynamic Objects

The whole idea of VR is to allow a user to navigate and interact with a VE. Thus when a user dons an HMD they will be tempted to reach out and touch some of the polygons and move them. This cannot happen unless the VE has been so constructed. For example, if the user wants to move specific vertices then they must be identified within the database during the modelling stage. It would be unusual to allow the user to modify all of the vertices as this could easily destroy the geometric integrity of the VE.

In the case of the user wanting to move an individual polygon or triangle, we must make sure that the polygon's edges are not shared by other polygons. If the edge is shared, then it cannot be moved, because it does not have an independent identity.

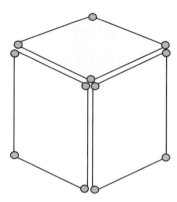

Figure 3.10   Three polygons with geometric independence.

Figure 3.10 shows three such polygons that are completely independent of one another.

When the user needs to move an entire object such as a chair, software tools are available to update the VE database with this knowledge. Thus when a user interacts with the VE within an immersive system, their virtual hand can be tested for a collision condition with the object. When a collision occurs, the user can instruct the system for the object to be moved to another position using hand gestures. For non-immersive systems a mouse is used to select an object and move it to a new position.

3.5 Constraints

Some objects in the VE may require being unconstrained, but others will require constraining in some form or another. For example, the chair shown in Fig. 3.11 could be constrained to rotate about its base, have an adjustable back, move freely across the floor, but prevented from being lifted off the floor. The handset of a virtual telephone, for example, must be unconstrained so that the user can lift it up and manipulate it freely. On the other hand, a door opening into a room requires to be constrained. In real life, a door is constrained by the action of its hinges and the door's frame, which prevents it from rotating indefinitely. If a virtual door is to behave like its real counterpart, it too, must be constrained to rotate through a specified angle.

Imagine a user immersed within a VE and sees a door in front of them. As they approach the door, their virtual hand collides with the coordinate geometry of the door. This is detected by the host computer and allows the user to open the door using appropriate hand gestures. And if the user attempts to open the door beyond its constrained angle, the system simply prevents the action from occurring. If this were not so, it would be mayhem – there would be chairs flying around the room, doors swinging indefinitely about their hinges, and tables embedded in the walls! Figure 3.12 shows how a wardrobe would have to be modelled and constrained to allow its doors and draws to be opened.

Figure 3.11   A virtual swivel chair. Image courtesy of James Hans.

Figure 3.12   A virtual wardrobe showing constraints on doors and draws. Images courtesy of James Hans.

3.6 Collision Detection

We have already come across the idea of virtual collisions, and perhaps now is a good time to explain how they work. To begin with, imagine a virtual teapot complete with spout, handle, and lid. It is probably constructed from 100 triangles, or so.

One method of implementing collision detection is to surround the teapot by an invisible box called a 'collision volume', which is stored alongside the teapot's surface geometry in the database. If we lift up the virtual teapot with collision detection activated the teapot can be moved about freely. However, if we bring the teapot too close to another object's collision volume, the host VR computer will detect the coordinates of the collision volumes touching or intersecting. When this occurs, any number of things could happen: to begin with, the intersection is prevented from happening, no matter how the user may force it to happen; the teapot's colour could change to indicate a collision has occurred; or the teapot could force the other object to move.

Now the idea of being able to move objects around a VE is very important, and the idea of allowing one object to collide with another opens up all sorts of possibilities. We will return to this matter later in the book – for now, though, let us continue with understanding more about collisions.

If the collision volume of the teapot is nothing more than a box, then we cannot expect a high level of realism when collisions occur. For example, if we slowly move the teapot towards a virtual cup and saucer, at some stage the collision volumes will touch. And if we continue to bring the teapot closer we will see the cup move away, even though the teapot and cup are not touching. Their collision volumes are touching, but not the polygons that make up the teapot and cup. In this trivial example we can cope with this visual error, but in a commercial engineering application it could be vital that the virtual objects must touch, rather than their collision volumes.

Figure 3.13 shows two trees and a pergola with their collision volumes not intersecting and intersecting. But even when the collision volumes intersect, the enclosed objects are not touching. If greater accuracy is required to detect collisions then a price has to be paid for its implementation. For example, instead of placing a collision volume around the entire object, collision volumes can be placed around individual elements. In the case of the teapot this could be the handle, spout, lid, and body. If this were not accurate enough, collision volumes could enclose individual polygons. And if this were not accurate enough, one could implement a strategy where collision detection was performed at a vertex and edge level. Figure 3.14 shows the four ways a pair of triangles can collide.

Now these different strategies require the host computer to do increasing levels of work comparing hundreds of thousands of coordinates, and at some stage it will become so great that it will slow down the system so much that it will be useless.

One can see that we are attempting to push computers to their limit, especially personal computers (PCs). But VR systems have to undertake a lot of work. They have to manipulate large databases of coordinates, support interaction, support collision detection, produce coloured pictures, monitor where the user's head and hand are in space, and maintain a real-time performance. If the system becomes 'jerky' because of inadequate processing power, then it can be intolerable. So although we would like high-fidelity images and physical realism, it is not always possible and a compromise has to be struck. For further information on collision detection see Kamat (1993).

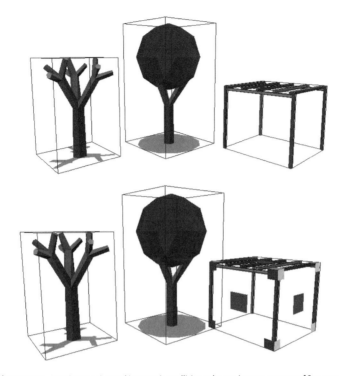

Figure 3.13   Non-intersecting and intersecting collision volumes. Images courtesy of Superscape.

Figure 3.14   Four ways two triangles can interact: vertex to plane, edge to edge, edge to plane, and vertex to vertex. A fifth possibility is plane to plane.

3.7 Perspective Views

Having looked at some of the issues associated with creating a VE using coordinates, let us see how it is possible to develop a perspective view of a VE.

Fortunately, this is very simple and even though the math is easy I will describe the process visually. If you wish to find out more about this subject, there are plenty of books available that explain how to perform this operation (Vince, 1995).

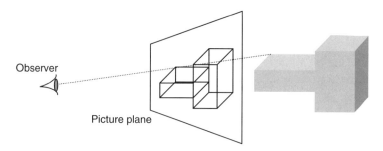

Figure 3.15   The objects on the right can be captured as a perspective image on the central picture plane by tracing lines back to the eye on the left.

To begin with, imagine you are in a room gazing outside through a window. Outside the building you can see trees, houses, roads, and clouds. If you wish to draw this view and show different features of the scene in perspective, then the following procedure can be used. First take a marker pen (a white board marker pen is preferable, especially if you wish to erase your masterpiece!) and stand at arm's length in front of the window and gaze straight ahead. Now without moving your head, draw upon the glass the scene outside. You will trace out contours and silhouettes of objects, and those objects further away from you will appear naturally smaller.

What you have drawn is a perspective view of the outside scene, and it would be similar to a photograph captured by a camera. Obviously, the view drawn on the window is influenced by your position in the building: the higher up you are, the more you see the tops of outside objects; the further away you are, the smaller the objects appear.

Now this drawing exercise is very simple to explain, and equally simple to implement within a computer. One simply projects the 3D database of coordinates through an imaginary window called the *picture plane* and convert them to a flat image as shown in Fig. 3.15. To obtain the different viewpoints the projection technique must know where the user's viewpoint is – but in a VR system this is always being monitored for this very purpose. For an immersive system, whenever the user moves his or her head, it is detected by the VR tracking system, which feeds it back to the computer. The computer, in turn, passes it onto the perspective software program that ensures that the user is always seeing an appropriate view. If there is any lag in the system, whether it is from the 3D tracker, or passing the data within the computer, the user sees images that appear a fraction of a second behind their head movements, which can be extremely distracting.

3.8 3D Clipping

When you are gazing through the window drawing the perspective scene, you can only see objects in front of you. Walls mask objects beyond your field of view (FOV), and your head masks objects behind you. This masking of unwanted information

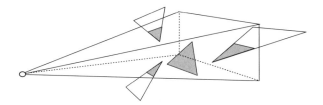

Figure 3.16 Clipping volume in the shape of a pyramid. Only the shaded parts of triangles are visible to the observer.

must be implemented within the computer, otherwise we will be overwhelmed by views of every object within the VE.

The process of removing unwanted detail is called *3D clipping*, and as this is another task for the computer, and is often implemented in hardware for high speed, rather than software. Figure 3.16 shows the clipping volume in the shape of a pyramid. In this case, only one triangle is completely visible to the observer, the other triangles are only partially visible, as indicated by the shaded areas.

Imagine, then, a VR user inside a virtual house. As the user gazes in one direction, objects behind the viewer are being clipped from their view. And if they turn around and face in the opposite direction they will see these objects, while the computer removes the previous ones from their view. If the user were now to float vertically through the ceiling towards the first floor, the clipping software will ensure that even when the user's head moves through the ceiling to emerge in a bedroom, all of the polygons are correctly clipped. Thus we can see that clipping is an important process as it enables us to pass miraculously through walls and ceilings without creating any spurious images.

3.9 Stereoscopic Vision

Most life forms have evolved with a pair of eyes – as two views give an increased FOV and also assist in the perception of depth. You may have experienced the excellent 3D effect that is created when looking at a pair of photographs through a stereoscope. As the two images are taken from two different positions in space, the brain uses these differences to create a single image that contains depth information. This is called *stereoscopic vision*.

Obviously, our own vision system is stereoscopic, and is something we take for granted. We depend on it to undertake the more tricky tasks such as threading a needle, sewing, fixing a nut onto a screw, etc. – tasks involving dexterity and precision. But we also depend on it, but to a lesser extent, to estimate the distance of an approaching car.

Stereoscopic vision is easily created within a VR system – we simply produce two views of the VE, one for the left eye, and the other for the right eye. This means that the perspective software must be given the distance between our eyes, which introduces the first problem. This distance changes from person-to-person, but a typical value of 6.5 cm will suffice. The software can now produce two distinct views of the VE that is, one 3.25 cm to the left of our gaze, and one 3.25 cm to the right. This increases further the work for the host computer, which now has two images to render!

Owing to this extra load for the computer, it is still usual to find monoscopic systems where the left and right eyes see the same image. Naturally, there is no depth information, and the user must learn how to interact without depth cues.

3.10 Rendering the Image

The next stage is to render the image in the form of pixels so it can be displayed upon a screen or HMD. There are several ways of achieving this: some techniques are very fast and produce an obvious 'computer look', whereas others take much longer but produce images that look like a real photograph. You can guess which technique is used in VR! It is not that we are deliberately trying to produce simple computer-generated images, that is, we are doing everything in our power to ensure that there is no unwanted lag or latency in the system. An immersive VR system is appalling if the latency extends to 0.25 s; therefore every thousandth of a second is vital. Ideally, one would like a VR system to be able to update the VE 50 times a second (50 Hz, pronounced Hertz), with a latency of no more than 50 ms.

3.10.1 Colour

Research has shown that the human eye samples the visible spectrum in three overlapping frequency bands with maximum sensitivities in the red, green, and blue (RGB) colours. These colours have been adopted as the three additive primary colours for mixing light sources, while yellow, cyan, and magenta are the corresponding subtractive primary colours for mixing paint pigment.

Computer technology uses mixtures of RGB to describe colour and it is convenient to specify a colour as three numbers that range from 0 to 1. Thus an RGB triplet of $0, 0, 0$ represents black, and $1, 1, 1$ represents white. Table 3.1 shows other values for RGB triplets and the corresponding colour, and Fig. 3.17 provides a spatial way of interpreting this RGB data.

Although a colour can be represented as an RGB triplet it is not very intuitive, and it is difficult to search for a specific colour simply by adding or subtracting different amounts of RGB. In an attempt to resolve this problem the hue, saturation, and value (HSV) colour space is also used to represent the quantities hue, saturation, and value. To begin with, a number between 0 and 1 determines a particular hue; then saturation, which also varies between 0 and 1, controls the amount of white light in the colour; and finally, value represents the brightness of the mixed colour.

Figure 3.18 illustrates the HSV colour space, and as both systems have their respective strengths, they are both used in user interfaces to describe colour.

Table 3.1	Values of RGB and the resulting colour.		
Red	Green	Blue	Colour
0	0	0	Black
0	0	1	Blue
0	1	0	Green
0	1	1	Cyan
1	0	0	Red
1	0	1	Magenta
1	1	0	Yellow
1	1	1	White

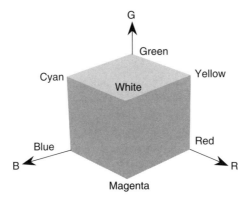

Figure 3.17   The RGB colour space.

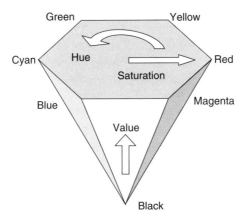

Figure 3.18   The HSV colour space.

3.10.2 Coloured Objects

After an object is modelled it is assigned a colour. This may be selected from a given palette of colours or a particular mix of the video primary colours: RGB. The entire model may have one colour, or it may be that different sides or polygons have specific colours, that is, virtually anything is possible.

You will probably know that a television screen is constructed from a matrix of discrete picture elements called *pixels*, and each pixel has a RGB phosphor dot. When three electron beams scan these pixels, the phosphors glow according to the intensity of the beams. This cathode ray tube (CRT) technology is only found in high-quality HMDs, and for everyday HMDs liquid crystal display (LCD) technology is used: it is lighter, cheaper, smaller, and readily available. Whether the display technology is CRT, LCD or video projectors, the images are represented as a matrix of pixels.

Before an image is displayed it is formed inside the computer's memory by the renderer program. While this process is underway, the previous image is being displayed. This overlapping of computer tasks is another method of keeping the VR system running as fast as possible.

The renderer uses the perspective view of an object to determine which pixels have to be updated, and the colour of the object is used to flood the relevant pixels. The image can be made to look life-like by colouring the object with colour shades that give the impression that it is lit by some light source. Another way is to let the renderer automatically work out the surface shading of the object. To do this, the renderer is given the position and intensity of a virtual light source, and using some simple laws of illumination, shades the object with acceptable colour intensities.

Shading algorithms range from the very simple to the very complex: Gouraud shading is found in most VR systems and renders polygons with subtle changes of intensity and colour over a polygon. The resultant image produces a matte effect, but is acceptable for most applications. Where it is important to see reflections of the illuminating light source Phong shading is used. This takes a little more time to compute but creates more realistic images, especially when the objects are supposed to be reflective. Plates 11 and 12 show two excellent examples of 3D modelling and rendering.

3.10.3 Light Sources

To add that extra degree of realism, a variety of light sources can be used to illuminate a VE. These include ambient, spot, fixed point, and parallel. Ambient light is a fixed background light level that has no direction, it means only colour and intensity. It is included in the lighting calculations as a constant term and can account for approximately 25% of the total illumination level. A virtual spotlight simulates the action of its real-world counterpart and has position, direction, spot angle, colour, and intensity. A fixed-point light source is a point in space that radiates light in all directions, and a parallel light source shines light in one direction as though it were located at some distant position like the sun. Together, these sources of light create realistic levels of illumination, but nowhere near as accurate as the radiosity technique.

Lights can be moved about the VE, and even attached to the user's hand to simulate a torch. And as long as the software system provides the facility, any parameter associated with a light can be altered.

As lights are represented as numerical quantities within a VR system, numbers can be positive and negative. A positive level of intensity represents a normal light source, but a negative value creates a source of darkness. Now this has no equal in the real world, but can be a useful rendering feature.

3.11 Rendering Algorithms

All renderers are faced with the problem of forming a picture in the frame-store such that objects mask one another correctly. In the field of computer graphics this is known as hidden-surface removal. A number of algorithms (techniques) have been developed over the years such as Z-buffering, the scan-line algorithm, painter's algorithm, ray tracing, the A-buffer, etc., and they all have strengths and weaknesses. In VR we are particularly interested in speed – for if it cannot run in real time, then it is of little use. I will describe the underlying principles of three of the above algorithms.

3.11.1 Painter's Algorithm

As the name suggests, this technique is similar to the way a painter creates a painting. For example, one would start painting the most distant elements such as the sky and horizon line, and over-paint these with objects that are closer to the painter. To implement this in software requires that we know how far each object is away from the viewer. This in itself is not too difficult, but in a VR system the user is continually moving about, and changes his or her relative position to every object. Therefore, it means that for every image, the software has to compute the distance of each object from the viewer; sort the distances in ascending sequence; and render the most distant one first, and the nearest last. This is the basic technique. What we now need are ways of speeding up the process to maximize the renderer's update rate.

A simple technique is to associate a bounding cube with every object. Although this exists in the database, it is never rendered, unless required for editing purposes. The system then sorts the bounding cubes into distance sequence, and starts by rendering the object whose bounding cube is furthest from the observer, and proceeds with closer and closer objects. For most situations the algorithm works very well, but as it is possible to enclose highly irregular objects by a simple cube, the algorithm is not 100% accurate. However, when such conflicts arise, a Z-buffer algorithm can be used to resolve the situation very effectively.

3.11.2 Scan-Line Algorithm

A video image is transmitted and displayed on a television screen in the form of horizontal rasters or scan lines, which is where the scan-line algorithm gets its name. The scan-line algorithm renders the image raster by raster, normally starting at the top, and working its way down to the bottom of the image.

To visualize what is happening, imagine gazing at a scene through a slit as shown in Fig. 3.19 that is as wide as the image but vertically very thin. The algorithm first

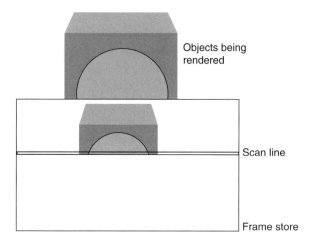

Figure 3.19   Rendering an image using the scan-line algorithm.

identifies the objects visible in the slit and proceeds to sort them in distance sequence and loads the raster of colours into the frame store. It then proceeds to the next raster down. But as this is so close to the scan line above, there is a very good chance that the same objects are visible, and therefore the distance relationships are the same. If another object comes into view, very little work is needed to adjust for its presence.

This algorithm has also been mixed with other techniques such as the Z-buffer, to create various hybrid renderers.

3.11.3 Z-Buffer

The *Z-buffer*, or *depth buffer* algorithm, avoids any kind of sorting by memorizing the depth of rendered polygons at a pixel level. Which means that if there are 640 × 480 pixels in the image, there is a corresponding piece of computer memory called the Z-buffer, to record the depth of the polygon covering each pixel. The letter Z is chosen, as it is the Z-axis that points away from the observer when the depth calculations are made.

To visualize how this works, imagine that the Z-buffer is primed with very large depth values, such as 10,000. Say the first polygon to be rendered is 500 units away, every pixel it covers will be rendered and the corresponding positions in the Z-buffer updated with the value 500. If the next polygon to be rendered is 1000 units away and is masked by the first polygon, the Z-buffer can be used to resolve the masking. For example, if the Z-buffer contains a depth value greater than 1000 then the new polygon is visible. If, on the other hand, it contains a depth value less than 1000, it means that a polygon has already been rendered that is closer. Figure 3.20 shows two views of portions of the Z-buffer. The left view shows the status of the buffer after the first polygon is rendered, and the right view shows the buffer after the second polygon is rendered.

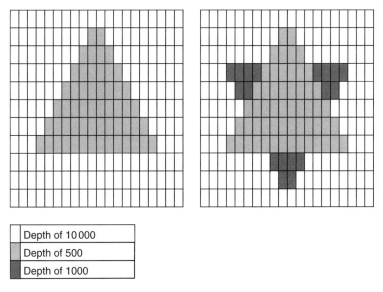

| Depth of 10 000 |
| Depth of 500 |
| Depth of 1000 |

Figure 3.20   The two images show how a Z-buffer records the depths of the two polygons.

As depth is maintained at a pixel level the Z-buffer can resolve interpenetrating objects. For example, if a small box intersected a larger sphere, the curves of intersection are revealed automatically by the Z-buffer, which saves an immense amount of modelling time.

Although the Z-buffer is effective at hidden-surface removal, the basic algorithm cannot cope with transparency and anti-aliasing. But the latter can be implemented approximately if the Z-buffer stores depths at sub-pixel level.

3.12 Texture Mapping

If further realism is required, such as reflections, shadows, and spotlights, more advanced techniques are required, which in turn require computers with more powerful graphics cards. However, one quick way of incorporating extra realism is with the aid of texture maps. These can be from photographs scanned into the computer or created by paint programs. For example, to make a virtual bookcase look more realistic, a photograph of wood grain can be scanned in and mapped onto the polygons by the renderer. Matching the scale of the texture to the size of the bookcase is important, and if the texture map is insufficient to cover a polygon, it can be repeated like a tile to ensure coverage. Figure 3.21 shows a wire frame and textured view of a bookcase. Figure 3.22 shows a texture map and the resulting effect when it is mapped onto a box.

Mapping texture on objects that remain close the observer is a very effective way of introducing extra detail, but problems arise when the object moves farther away. For example, if the object's size reduces by a factor of 5, the original texture is far too

Figure 3.21   A wire frame and textured virtual bookcase. Images courtesy of James Hans.

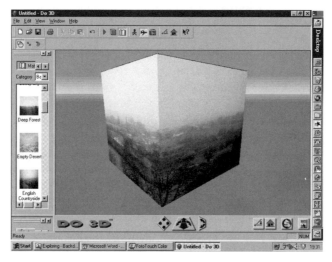

Figure 3.22   Planar texture map and its mapping onto a box.

detailed. And if the size reduces by a factor of 10, another level of texture detail is required. This problem was appreciated by Williams (1983) who proposed that a set of texture maps could be used to decorate objects at different distances. The name *MIP mapping* or *MIP textures* is given to this strategy. MIP textures also minimize aliasing artefacts that arise when *texels* (texture pixels) are mapped onto screen pixels.

3.12.1 Billboard Textures

When a texture map is used as a backdrop to a scene, such as the one shown in Fig. 3.22, it is called a *billboard texture*. This technique is also used to introduce trees into a scene. A single vertical polygon is placed in a scene, onto which is mapped a photograph of a tree. The trees in Fig. 3.23 are all billboard textures. If we moved around such a tree, we would not discover any depth to the texture, because it is nothing more than a photograph. In IGs, the viewer never sees a side view of the tree, because the tree's polygon is automatically rotated to face the viewer. One would expect that such a trick would be easy to detect, but when the viewer is engaged in some training task, it is unnoticed.

3.12.2 Dynamic Textures

Dynamic textures are a sequence of texture maps applied to a surface in quick succession, and are used to simulate special effects such as flames, explosions, and smoke trails.

3.13 Bump Mapping

Another way of increasing image realism is *bump mapping* and was developed by Blinn (1978). Basically, it consists of using a texture map to modulate the way light is reflected pixel by pixel. One would normally use photographs of bumpy materials such as concrete, leather, orange peel, etc. lit obliquely. Real-time IGs use the technique to create sea states, as shown in Fig. 3.24.

3.14 Environment Mapping

Environment mapping simulates the effect of polished surfaces that reflect their surroundings. To a certain extent, it is similar to texture mapping, but an environment map is not fixed to the object's surface – it moves whenever the observer moves to create the impression of a reflection. It is particularly useful in the display of car bodies, and shows how reflective highlights travel on the surface of a moving car.

An environment map may be produced from a collection of photographs, which capture a 360° view of a specific scene. Plates 15 and 16 show two such maps. The spherical distortion in the maps disappears in the rendering stage when the maps are

Figure 3.23   Real-time textured scene. Image courtesy of Evans & Sutherland Computer Corporation, Salt Lake City, Utah, USA.

Figure 3.24   Real-time bump mapping. Image courtesy of Evans & Sutherland Computer Corporation, Salt Lake City, Utah, USA.

reflected in some reflective surface. The final effect helps to convince the viewer that the objects are real because they reflect their environment, which is photo-realistic.

3.15 Shadows

Shadows in the real world just happen, but virtual shadows require considerable levels of computation. This is rather unfortunate because shadows do play an important role in the way we interpret the position and orientation of objects in the real world.

Various techniques have been developed to compute shadows, and they all require a geometric analysis of the spatial relationship between light sources and the objects in a scene. Ray tracing is particularly good at creating shadows, so too is radiosity, but at the moment, neither can be used in real time. However, when a high-performance graphics computer is available, it is possible to compute shadows for some scenes in real time.

As shadows are so important, simple techniques have been developed to introduce some form of a shadow, even though the end result is not perfect. One such technique used in flight simulators and certain computer games consists of sliding a shadow polygon over the ground in synchronization with the motion of an object. Plates 1, 2, 7, and 8 show how effective computer-generated shadows can be.

3.16 Radiosity

There are two rendering techniques that create photo-realistic images: ray tracing and radiosity. Ray tracing is excellent for realizing shadows, reflections, refraction, etc., but is still too slow for VR systems. Plates 7 and 8 show ray-traced views of an aircraft interior, while Plates 5 and 6 show views of a restaurant. Radiosity is an equally slow technique but produces wonderful views of interiors as shown in Fig. 2.2, Fig. 3.25 and Plates 4 and 13. It achieves this by simulating the internal reflections that arise when an interior is illuminated by light sources. These are represented as a series of simultaneous equations that are solved to find a common solution, which can take anything from a few seconds, minutes or hours – much depends on the complexity of the model.

Progressive refinement is another way of solving the radiosity model. It begins by looking at the brightest source of light and distributes its energy throughout the model. It then selects the next brightest source and continues to repeat the algorithm until changes in the image are too small to notice.

If the technique takes so long, why are we looking at it if there is no chance of it running in real time? Radiosity is relevant to VR for the following reason: once the algorithm has been used to compute the delicate shades and shadows within a VE, the colour intensities can be stored and associated with the individual polygons. From then on, there is no need for any virtual light source – the light intensities and shadows have been 'frozen' onto the polygons, and it is possible to move about the VE in real time. However, if we move an object in the VE it takes with it the original

Figure 3.25 Radiosity interior of a car. Image courtesy of LightWork Design. Produced using the LightWorks rendering system.

shading, and leaves behind shadows that may have been cast upon a floor or wall. For many applications, especially those where VR is being used for visualization purposes, this is a small price to pay for excellent image quality.

Plate 13 shows a beautiful scene rendered using the LightWorks rendering system. It incorporates reflections that have been calculated using ray tracing, which would not be used if the model were to be used in a VR system, because they are viewer dependent.

3.16.1 Fog

Fog or haze has been used in flight simulator IGs for many years. A simple solution is to fade the colour of objects at a certain distance into a gray to give the impression of a background haze. But modern IGs can simulate fog very realistically and simulate the effect of ground fog settling in valleys. Figure 3.26 shows a real-time image from an Evans & Sutherland IG.

3.16.2 Transparency

Although most objects are opaque, it is essential to be able to simulate transparent materials such as glass, water, and certain plastics. Although this can be done, it does

Figure 3.26   Real-time image of realistic fog. Image courtesy of Evans & Sutherland Computer Corporation, Salt Lake City, Utah, USA.

have an impact on the renderer. The Z-buffer technique, for example, renders objects in an arbitrary sequence. And if a transparent object is rendered first, followed by an opaque object, once the transparent object is completed, no information remains to compute how much of the opaque object will be visible. Other types of renderer require access to all of the objects – transparent and opaque – in order that transparency calculations can be made. In VR systems, one has the opportunity of declaring that an object is coloured with a certain degree of transparency.

As light travels slower in materials such as glass and water, its direction changes and gives rise to refraction. It is possible to calculate such phenomena using ray tracing, but this, at the moment, cannot be achieved in real time.

3.17 Other Computer Graphics Techniques

Computer graphics consists of many more techniques that will eventually become part of VR. Some of the relevant ones include soft objects, particle systems, non-uniform rational B-spline (NURBs), depth of field, and volumetric rendering.

3.17.1 Soft Objects

The majority of objects used in computer graphics are modelled as a boundary skin, and the technique is called *boundary representation* or *B-Rep*. This boundary normally has a polygonal form and is based on measurements for some physical object. It is also possible to express 3D shapes mathematically. For example, the equation of a sphere reminds us that $radius^2 = x^2 + y^2 + z^2$, where the point (x, y, z) is any point on the sphere's surface. Thus for a given radius, it is possible to find a range of values for x, y, and z that satisfy this equation. The next problem is connecting these points into a polygonal boundary representation. The interesting thing is that if equations can be used to model shapes then it is possible to utilize a wide range of mathematical surfaces. For example, we could use the equations used for describing electric and magnetic fields; we could even use equations that described the surface geometry of a drop of water. Such objects are called *soft objects*, because the objects are very rarely rigid. Figure 3.9 shows a variety of 3D primitives, but in the foreground it is a soft object formed from two close spheres. Using this technique it is possible to animate two individual spheres colliding with one another and creating one larger sphere.

3.17.2 Particle Systems

Particle systems are used to model large number of points that can be animated to simulate droplets of water, fire, explosions, clouds, and other natural phenomena. They have been used for some time in flight simulators to simulate snow, and they can be animated to reproduce the same visual effect when driving through a snowstorm using landing lights. Each particle is given a position in space, colour and lifetime, and by changing these parameters it is possible to reproduce a wide variety of effects that could not be achieved using polygons.

3.17.3 NURBs

A *NURB* is a mathematical curve widely used in CAD to describe complex surfaces such as those found on car bodies. They are a very powerful modelling tool and enable a designer to describe a surface in terms of a few curves that can be blended to form a smooth continuous surface. A NURB is created using a set of control points, and as the control points are adjusted the NURB responds by forming a new smooth curve.

3.17.4 Depth of Field

The majority of computer-generated images have an infinite depth of field, where every object in the scene is in perfect focus. In reality we know that this does not happen due to the optical structure of the human eye. As we have become accustomed to focusing on an object and noticing that the foreground and background are out of focus, it would be useful to simulate this effect. Using ray tracing it is possible to introduce depth of field in computer images, but unfortunately not in real time.

3.17.5 Volumetric Rendering

The shading techniques, such as Gouraud's and Phong's shadings, are very simple shaders and only approximate to what happens in reality. Ray tracing and radiosity are much more accurate techniques, but require substantially more time to render a scene. Volumetric rendering simulates another type of natural phenomena that occurs when light intersects a volume of space containing dust, smoke or mist. The technique is very effective and makes computer-generated images much more believable.

3.18 Summary

We have seen that computer graphics consists of a variety of techniques concerned with modelling 3D objects and VEs, assigning physical attributes, obtaining a perspective view, and colouring the image. These are standard techniques that have been used in computer animation and CAD for many years. However, these and other applications have never had to work in real time – users have been prepared to wait for anything from a few seconds to a couple of hours for a single image. VR has no choice but to work in real time and this means that ultra-fast, computer graphics techniques have to be found to keep latency to a minimum. It is easy to understand why it is difficult to run such techniques in real time, for if we are attempting to update a VE at 25 Hz, there is only 40 ms to create each image, which is very small, even in the time span of a computer.

Unfortunately, there has not been space to go any deeper into these techniques, however, what has been covered is sufficient to understand the role of computer graphics in VR.

4

Human Factors

4.1 Introduction

Before proceeding with the technology of virtual reality (VR) it will be useful to explore aspects of ourselves that will be influenced by this technology – this area is known as *human factors* and covers a wide range of interesting but complex topics.

Human factors cover much more than the physical aspects addressed in this chapter. It embraces issues such as:

- human learning in virtual environments (VEs);
- spatial cognition, spatial memory, and spatial ability in VEs;
- individual differences in VEs;
- cognitive models for VEs;
- multi-user VE design methods;
- social interaction within VEs.

These topics, unfortunately, are beyond the scope of this text as researchers around the world are still addressing them, so I will just look at our senses.

The senses for vision, hearing, smell, taste, and equilibrium are the normal *special senses*; whereas the senses for tactile, position, heat, cold, and pain are the *somatic senses*. In this chapter however, we will look only at some relevant facts related to the sensory systems exploited by VR technologies. These include vision, hearing, tactile, and equilibrium.

Readers who wish to discover more about this interesting subject are recommended to refer to Guyton's *Textbook of Medical Physiology* (1991).

4.2 Vision

It is obvious that our visual system is an essential human factor to be taken into account when designing VR hardware and software. The eye and the mechanism of vision is complex, and we have still a long way to go in understanding how the eye and brain work together, not to mention the act of seeing. Fortunately, we do not need to know too much about how the eye functions – just enough to understand how it can be best exploited without being abused.

4.2.1 The Eye

The eye is a sphere enclosing a lens that focuses light on the light-sensitive retina fixed to the back of the eyeball. From the retina, signals are processed and transported via the optic nerve to the visual cortex where the action of seeing is organized. Light first enters the eye through the transparent *cornea*, and then through a hole called the *pupil* before being refracted by the lens to focus on the retina (see Fig. 4.1). But because light is coming from objects at incredible distances such as the moon (400,000 km) and from hand-held objects only a few centimetres away, the lens must be able to automatically adjust its refractive power to keep images in focus. This is called *accommodation* and is achieved by contracting and relaxing the ciliary muscles surrounding the lens.

4.2.2 Colour Receptors

The retina contains two types of light-sensitive cells called *rods* and *cones*. The rods are sensitive to low levels of illumination and are active in night vision; however, they do not contribute towards our sense of colour – this is left to the cone cells that are sensitive to three overlapping regions of the visible spectrum: red, green, and blue (RGB). Collectively, they sample the incoming light frequencies and intensities, and give rise to nerve impulses that eventually end up in the form of a coloured image.

The *fovea* is the centre of the retina and is responsible for capturing fine-coloured detail – the surrounding area is still sensitive to colour but at a reduced spatial resolution. The fovea enables us to perform tasks such as reading, and if we attempt to read

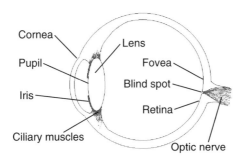

Figure 4.1   The human eye.

outside of this area, the image is too blurred to resolve any useful detail. The fovea is only 0.1 mm in diameter, which corresponds to approximately 1° of the eye's field of view (FOV). Towards the edge of the retina the cells become very sensitive to changes in light intensity, and provide peripheral vision for sensing movement.

4.2.3 Visual Acuity

Acuity is a measure of the eye's resolving power, and because the density of cells varies across the retina, measurements are made at the fovea. An average eye can resolve two bright points of light separated 1.5 mm at a distance of 10 m. This corresponds to 40 s or arc, and is equivalent to a distance of 2 μm on the retina.

4.2.4 The Blind Spot

The brain is connected to each eye via an optic nerve that enters through the back of the eye to connect to the retina. At the point of entry the distribution of rods and cones is sufficiently disturbed to create an area of blindness called the *blind spot*, but this does not seem to cause us any problems. The blind spot is easily identified by a simple experiment. To begin with, close one eye – for example the right eye – then gaze at some distant object with the left eye. Now hold up your left-hand index finger at arm's length slightly left of your gaze direction. While still looking ahead, move your index finger about slowly. You will see the finger tip vanish as it passes over the blind spot. What is strange, is that although the image of the finger disappears, the background information remains! It is just as well that this does not create problems for us in the design of head-mounted displays (HMDs).

4.2.5 Stereoscopic Vision

If we move towards an object, the ciliary muscles adjust the shape of the lens to accommodate the incoming light waves to maintain an in-focus image. Also, the eyes automatically converge to ensure that the refracted images fall upon similar areas of the two retinas. This process of mapping an image into corresponding positions upon the two retinas is the basis of *stereoscopic vision*. The difference between the retinal images is called *binocular disparity* and is used to estimate depth, and ultimately gives rise to the sense of three dimensional (3D) (see Fig. 4.2).

4.2.6 Stereopsis Cues

In 1832 Charles Wheatstone showed that a 3D effect could be produced by viewing two two-dimensional (2D) images using his stereoscope. Brewster went onto perfect the device using prisms instead of the mirrors used by Wheatsone. The 3D image formed by two separate views, especially those provided by the eyes, enable us to estimate the depth of objects, and such cues are called *stereopsis cues*.

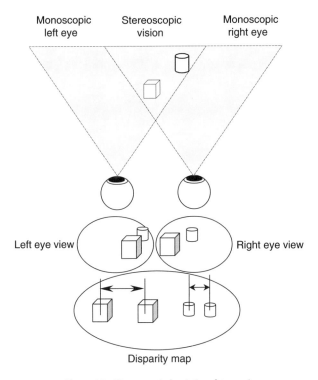

Figure 4.2 Diagrammatic description of stereopsis.

It had been assumed that stereoscopic perception was linked to our knowledge of an object, but in 1971 Julesz showed that it was in fact independent. By viewing patterns of random dots in a stereoscope Julesz was able to show that when the patterns where displaced horizontally, the brain used the image disparity to create 3D depth. The fact that the dot patterns were random showed that the brain did not require knowledge of the image to perceive a 3D effect. Since then random dot stereograms have been available commercially, and although they only consist of a single poster, when viewed carefully, a 3D effect is seen.

An HMD is nothing more than a stereoscope, but instead of photographs animated video images are used. What is essential though, is that the views seen by the two eyes must overlap – and it is in this area of overlap that stereoscopic vision is perceived. Figure 4.2 shows this diagrammatically, and because the illustrated cube is closer than the cylinder, its image disparity is greater.

4.2.7 Motion Parallax Cues

Although stereopsis is a very efficient strategy for estimating the depth of objects, the brain has learned that it is always best to have an alternative strategy. In this case, *motion parallax cues* are also used to estimate the depth of moving objects, and uses image speed across the retina as a cue. Furthermore, where stereopsis uses both eyes to compute the disparity between the two views of an object, motion parallax only requires one eye. An object close to the eye will appear to sweep out a large angle across the retina, whereas a distant object will not only be smaller, but it will move through a smaller angle.

4.2.8 Perspective Depth Cues

Perspective depth cues arise when we are familiar with the normal size of an object. For example, when we see a large plane such as a Boeing 767 flying, its small size confirms that it is a considerable distance away – for we know that on the ground its size is overwhelming.

The brain does not rely on one strategy to determine an object's depth – whatever cues are available, whether in the form of motion parallax cues, stereopsis cues, or perspective cues – they all contribute towards a collective answer.

4.2.9 Binocular Visual Field

Our two eyes produce two overlapping fields of view that create a binocular visual field of approximately $\pm 90°$ horizontally and $\pm 60°$ vertically. The area of overlap is about 120°, where stereopsis occurs. For example, if we gaze ahead we are aware that our central FOV is rich in colour, and objects are located precisely in space. However, if we fixate upon some central feature of the scene, it is very difficult to distinguish the form of objects positioned at the limit of our peripheral vision. There is no depth sensation and limited colour information, but moving objects are easily perceived.

Looking at the world through one eye is still interesting, but one cannot deny the sense of presence that arises when we open the other eye. Stereoscopic vision provides that overwhelming sense of being part of the world that a single eye can never provide. And it is this sense of presence that VR is attempting to mimic through stereoscopic HMDs. However, creating a realistic, wide-angle, binocular visual field is a real technical challenge, which is why cave automation virtual environments (CAVEs) and panoramic screens are popular.

4.2.10 Image Processing

The eye is not just an organic camera, and the way we perceive the world is not just a question of optics. We are endowed with very sophisticated image processing facilities to recognize human faces, the depth of objects, and whether something is upside down or not. For example, because the sun is always above the ground, objects tend to be illuminated at the top, and in shadow at the bottom. Our visual system has adapted to this natural phenomenon and uses it to extract information about the orientation of objects.

4.2.11 Persistence of Vision

When we accidentally look at a bright light, an after image can stay with us for some seconds. This is because the retina becomes saturated and requires time to restore the normal levels of chemicals. Apart from this electrochemical latency, our short-term visual memory can hold onto an image long after we close our eyes. This *persistence of vision* enables a series of discrete images repeated at a certain speed to be perceived as continuous. This is called the *critical fusion frequency* (CFF) and depends on the image brightness, and is around 20 Hz.

4.2.12 Flicker

Persistence of vision is exploited by television and computer displays by refreshing the screen many times a second. The refresh field rate for television is 50 Hz for the UK and 60 Hz for the USA, but some manufacturers have doubled these rates to reduce flicker even further. Flicker can be very tiresome, and in some cases can seriously interfere with the actions of our brain. For example, driving along a tree-lined road with a low sun can be highly dangerous, as the strobing of light and dark can induce an epileptic fit in some people.

4.3 Vision and Display Technology

From this brief description we see that our eyes are constantly working to ensure that we capture anything that could be useful to our survival. However, it is not too difficult to appreciate that our eyes have to behave differently when we don an HMD. To begin with, they are unable to focus on different objects within the VE – for all objects are in clear focus and all light rays come from the same distance. There are optical distortions that in no way contribute towards creating a sense of presence, and there are physiological problems that arise from conflicts in accommodation and convergence.

4.3.1 Optical Distortions

The optical distortions found in HMDs arise from the optical elements used to collimate the image. Such distortions include *astigmatism*, *barrel*, and *pincushion distortion*, and *chromatic* and *spherical aberrations*. Non-spherical lenses introduce a double image when a point is viewed off axis; this is called astigmatism. Barrel and pincushion distortion are when the optical system becomes non-linear either horizontally or vertically, and their effects are shown in Fig. 4.3. Chromatic aberration is when light of different wavelengths focuses at different points, and is removed by an achromatic lens combination. And spherical aberration is due to changes in focal length across the diameter of a lens.

4.3.2 Collimation Distance

The lens combination placed in front of the liquid crystal display (LCD) or the cathode ray tube (CRT) units determines the distance at which the image appears to be

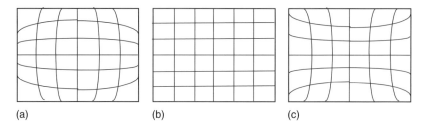

(a)   (b)   (c)

Figure 4.3   (a) Barrel, (b) no, and (c) pincushion distortions.

located, and is known as the *collimation distance*. In certain flight simulator displays the collimation distance approximates to infinity. In fact, this is a theoretical value – in practice it varies between several hundred metres to several thousand metres. Either way, the images appear to be located at a great distance.

In real life, light waves travelling from a distant mountain have a large radius of curvature when they arrive at our eyes. Whereas, the radius of curvature of light waves emanating from a nearby object is considerably smaller. It is this difference in curvature that requires the eye's lens to change shape if near and far objects are to be seen in focus. Now if we look into a display system collimated to infinity, our eyes will relax to accommodate the image. And because the light appears to come from infinity, there is a natural expectation for the image content to contain appropriate objects associated with a distant landscape. If however, we attempt to display an object that should appear relatively close, there is an immediate conflict. The motion parallax cues are wrong; eye convergence is minimal; and our ciliary muscles are relaxed. The overall sensation is very strange and still causes some problems for the flight simulation industry.

The reverse can be found in HMDs. If these are collimated to 2 or 3 m say, it is difficult to display distant objects with any realism. However, given a little time, we can adapt to these anomalies.

4.3.3 Depth of Field

In the real world, we perceive objects located at different distances, because the light waves reaching our eyes have different radii of curvature. Within a certain tolerance there is a depth of field that is in focus – objects that are before or beyond this zone are out of focus. This is a useful feature of our visual system as it permits us to concentrate on specific objects without being distracted by unwanted information.

Currently, display technology cannot collimate at a pixel level – the entire image is collimated at one distance; and although it is possible to adjust to this effect it is not an ideal solution. It is fortuitous that the Z-buffer rendering technique employs a depth buffer to store the depth detail for every pixel. Hopefully, one day, it will be possible to exploit this information to develop an HMD with a true depth of field.

One of the biggest disappointments of early VR systems was the HMDs. Their resolution was so poor that individual pixels were visible, and the optical sensation was similar to looking through two cardboard tubes! Attempting to create a real sensation of presence within the VE was very difficult, as one was constantly aware of the imperfections of the HMD. Today, although very high-quality display devices exist that provide excellent resolution (see Appendix B), an HMD does not exist that in any way matches the technical specification of our own visual system.

4.4 Hearing

Sound, like colour, is a creation of the brain. Pressure waves that impinge upon our ears give rise to an amazing spectrum of auditory sensations that provide a medium for speech and music, not to mention the everyday noises from trains, cars, telephones, and alarm bells.

4.4.1 The Ear

For our purposes it is convenient to divide the ear into three parts: the *outer ear*, *middle ear*, and the *inner ear*. The outer ear consists of the *pinna*, which we normally call the ear (see Fig. 4.4). It has quite a detailed shape and plays an important role in capturing sound waves, but more importantly, it shapes the spectral envelope of incident sound waves. This characteristic will be explored further when we examine sound direction.

The middle ear consists of the *tympanic membrane* (the eardrum) and the *ossicular system*, which conducts sound vibrations to the inner ear via a system of interconnecting bones. The *cochlea* is located in the inner ear, and is responsible for discriminating loudness and frequency. Finally, signals from the cochlea are interpreted by the brain's auditory cortex as the sensation of sound.

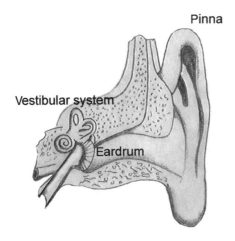

Figure 4.4   Sketch of the human ear.

4.4.2 Speed, Frequency, Wavelength, and Volume

Sound waves travel through any solid, gas, or liquid, and for each medium there is a speed of propagation. In air, the speed is approximately 344 m/s, which is very slow compared to the speed of light – 300,000 km/s! Where different frequencies of light give rise to sensations of colour, different frequencies of sound are detected as changes in pitch. It is the subtle mixture of frequencies that make up the different sounds we associate with objects such as a piano, violin, drum, or a wine glass being hit by a spoon.

A young person's auditory frequency range extends approximately from 20 to 20,000 cycles per second (c/s), but as we age, this can reduce to 50–8000 c/s. If one visualizes a sound wave as a cyclic disturbance of air molecules moving forward and backward, the wavelength of the sound wave is the distance between the two corresponding points in successive cycles, and is different for different frequencies (see Fig. 4.5). For example, at a frequency of 20 c/s, the wavelength is 17.2 m; and at 20,000 c/s the wavelength reduces to 17.2 mm. However, these distances are not fixed, because the velocity of sound in air depends on its temperature.

The amplitude of the pressure waves controls the sound volume, and the ear is particularly adept in detecting the faintest whisper to the most intense explosion. This range of sound intensities results in oscillations in the inner ear with an amplitude ratio of 1 to 1 million. However, this difference in sound level eventually gets compressed to a 10,000-fold change.

4.4.3 Direction

When a door bangs shut, pressure waves spread through the air and eventually impinge upon our ears. Perhaps, the left ear may detect the pressure waves before the right ear, and as our ears are approximately 20 cm apart, a time delay of 0.6 ms arises, that can be detected by the brain's auditory cortex. This obviously is something the brain uses to assist in locating the horizontal source of the sound, but it does not explain how we locate the source in the vertical plane. The interaction of the sound wave with our head and the pinnae play a significant role in shaping its spectral content.

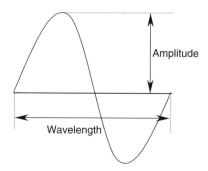

Figure 4.5   Amplitude and wavelength of a waveform.

Sounds from different directions are influenced differently by the geometry of our head and ears, and our brains are able to exploit this interaction to localize the sound source. This is easily demonstrated by 'cupping' one's hands and placing them close to one's ears – ambient sounds are immediately 'coloured'. If our 'cupped' hands have this effect upon sounds, it is only natural that our ears must modify the spectral characteristics before the waves travel towards the inner ear. Research by Shaw (1974) confirmed this phenomenon, and showed that the spectral shaping was dependent on the spatial origin of the sound source.

4.4.4 Sound Stage

When we look at the real world we are convinced that what we see is physically independent on us and that we are a natural part of it. For example, as I look through my office window I can see trees and houses and I like to believe that what I see is out there. But we know that this is not so – what we see is experienced *inside* our brain. Somewhere within our brain we are creating a 'visual stage' built from signals from our eyes, memories, expectations, etc.

Now when we listen to a stereo-hi-fi system we sit equidistant between the two speakers and an appropriate distance away. And because our left and right ears receive different signals, our auditory cortex is able to reconstruct a *sound stage* of the music that has spatial breadth and depth. But this sound stage does not appear to be inside our heads – it appears to exist in the space occupied by the speakers. However, we know that this cannot be so. Just like our sense of vision, our sense of sound must occur within our brain. What actually happens is that, spatially, our sound stage overlays our visual stage, and sounds are accurately correlated with physical objects.

Research by Plenge (1974) showed that the pinnae were actually responsible for externalizing the sound stage. For when the influence of the pinnae was removed, the sound stage appeared to be internal, rather than external. This is easily demonstrated by the action of modern lightweight headphones that 'plug' into the middle ear. When wearing these headphones, one is aware that the stereo-sound stage exists between the ears, and does not have any external existence.

It was quickly realized that if the signals driving a set of headphones could be artificially modified to simulate the spectral shaping by the head and the pinnae, it would be possible to externalize the sound stage. Indeed this is the case, and the signal processing functions required are called *head-related transfer functions* (HRTFs). For accuracy, the HRTFs take into account the shape of the upper torso. Furthermore, as the shape of our ears, head, and shoulders are all different; we each possess a personal set of HRTFs.

Now the reason for explaining this process is that VR systems are often equipped with stereo-headphones that can be used to communicate sound signals from virtual objects. If these signals are not pre-processed by HRTFs, the sound stage will appear within the user's head rather than superimposed on the external visual stage. However, the HRTFs will probably be based on some generic set of pinnae, head and torso measurements, and the effect is only approximate.

4.5 Tactile

The tactile senses are important in VR as it would be useful to touch virtual objects, feel them vibrate, and react to their weight. Obviously, such sensations have to be simulated, and it will be useful to understand some of the sensory mechanisms involved.

4.5.1 Touch Receptors

Touch, pressure, and vibration are *somatic senses* that are nervous mechanisms for collecting sensory data from our body. All three sensations are detected by similar types of receptors: touch receptors are found in the skin or in local tissue; pressure receptors lie within deeper tissues and respond to tissue deformation; and the sensation of vibration is detected by both touch and pressure receptors. Guyton (1991) classifies the somatic sensations as follows:

> *Exteroreceptive sensations* are those from the surface of the body. *Proprioceptive sensations* are those having to do with the physical state of the body, including position sensations, tendon and muscle sensations, pressure sensations from the bottom of the feet, and even the sensation of equilibrium, which is generally considered to be a 'special' sensation rather than a somatic sensation.

> *Visceral sensations* are those from the viscera of the body; in using this term one usually refers specifically to sensations from the internal organs.

> The *deep sen*sations are those that come from the deep tissues, such as from fasciae, muscles, bone, and so forth. These include mainly 'deep' pressure, pain and vibration.

The tactile senses present much more of a challenge to VR technology than any of the other senses. For if we are to stimulate the tactile senses we have to find ways of stimulating the skin and deep muscle tissue. The tactile receptors comprise free nerve endings that are found all over the surface of the skin and within certain tissues. The slightest breeze or a fly landing for a fraction of a second can activate these.

Where spatial discrimination is required and touch sensation is vital, a receptor called *Meissner's corpuscles* is used. These are found especially on the lips and fingertips. Hairy areas of the skin contain *expanded tip tactile receptors* which adapt slowly to their stimuli – this allows them to monitor touch conditions that remain over a period of time.

Each hair on our skin has a nerve fibre attached to its base called the *hair end-organ*. These are stimulated just before our skin makes contact with a foreign object. Deeper inside the skin and tissue are located *Ruffini's end-organs* that respond to continuous states of deformation, continuous touch conditions, and pressure signals. And finally, *pacinian corpuscles* are located just beneath the skin and deep within the facial tissues; these are sensitive to tissue vibrations.

With such an array of receptors, it is going to be difficult to stimulate them using electronic and mechanical technologies. Even the act of wearing a glove containing active pressure pads will stimulate the skin receptors. We may be able to sense the vibrations emanating from the glove, but it cannot be compared to holding or touching a real object.

If we are to feel the weight of a virtual object, somehow forces must be transmitted to our arms. But it is not just our arms that react to the weight of something – it is our whole body. Even our legs and the soles of our feet respond to the weight.

4.6 Equilibrium

In the previous section on hearing we saw that the inner ear houses the cochlea, which converts sound pressure waves into nerve signals. The inner ear is also the home for the *vestibular system*, which is the sense for equilibrium. The vestibular system informs the brain whether we are standing upright or leaning to one side; whether we are stationary or accelerating; and in general, helps the brain understand our relationship with the ground. However, our ability to stand upright and maintain balance is also supported by complementary systems of muscles that respond to the pull of gravity.

The spinal cord connects to the brain at the brain stem, which is responsible for controlling various motor and sensory functions such as equilibrium, eye movement, gastrointestinal function, automatic body movements, and respiration and control of the cardiovascular system. In general, these primitive functions can operate without any intervention from the higher levels of the brain. It is also interesting to note that when we loose equilibrium – for whatever reason – these motor functions become excited; heart and respiration rate changes, vision becomes unstable, and our stomachs respond with dramatic effect! But more of this later.

4.6.1 The Vestibular Apparatus

The *vestibular apparatus* functions by detecting the motion of fluid stored in various chambers and ducts as shown in Fig. 4.4. The *utricle* and *saccule* chambers are responsible for measuring the head's orientation relative to the earth's gravitational field. They achieve this by monitoring the excitation of small hairs by a sticky liquid that moves whenever we bend our head forward, backward, or sideways.

The three *semicircular ducts* are hollow semicircular bones organized at 90° to one another, that enables them to sense motion in 3D. When we rotate our head, liquid inside the ducts is displaced and small hairs are excited, but within a second or so, the liquid catches up with the motion of the duct. Similarly, when we stop our head rotating, the same hairs are excited. Thus the semicircular ducts act as accelerometers and are sensitive to about 1°/s/s; but they do *not* detect if equilibrium has been lost. Owing to their sensitivity, their true role is to 'advise' the brain that equilibrium *will* be lost if action is not taken. This gives the brain, time to respond with appropriate muscular adjustments throughout the body, reflexive arm gestures, and rotation of the eyes to retain a stable image. It is a beautiful arrangement, but for some, it is easily disturbed.

4.6.2 Motion Sickness

Many people are sensitive to certain types of motion and suffer from the effects of motion sickness. This begins with a strange sense of 'something's wrong'; moves through stages of sweating, nausea, loss of balance, and can eventually end with vomiting, followed by a long period of 'being out of action'. All of this is attributed to a loss of equilibrium.

Seasickness is a common complaint when sailing on rough seas. For some people though, the sea does not have to be particularly rough – just losing sight of the horizon for a few seconds is sufficient to induce nausea. Other people are ill when flying, being driven in a car, or sitting the wrong way in a moving train. But it is also known that people who spend too long in flight simulators, especially those systems with panoramic displays and no motion platform, suffer similar problems. Some pilots who undergo long training sessions in dome simulators report 'out-of-body' experiences, loss of balance, and general disorientation, and require a good 24-h period of readjustment.

4.6.3 Implications for VR

Users of VR systems must also be aware of the problems introduced by the technology of HMDs, immersive displays, motion platforms, and real-time computer graphics, as they can all unwittingly induce motion sickness. Take, for example, HMDs. These cut the user from the real visual world, and thus isolate them from landmarks such as the ground plane, and the horizon. An HMD's optical system must be aligned correctly. For example, if the right-hand image is slightly rotated relative to the left-hand image, one eye will attempt to resolve the situation by rotating about its gaze axis. This not only causes eyestrain, but also can induce serious nausea.

Large immersive panoramic displays envelop our horizontal FOV, and can induce motion sickness when viewing certain types of graphics. This is because these displays stimulate our peripheral FOV where motion cues are detected. If the real-time images involve rapid rotations and sudden stops and starts, motion sickness can be induced within seconds.

The motion platforms used in flight and entertainment simulators are able to slide along and rotate about three axes; such movements are called *degrees of freedom* (DOF). Some motion platforms are constrained to 3 DOF, whereas others are unconstrained and possess 6 DOF. Figure 4.6 shows the three axes oriented such that one-axis points forward, another points upward, and the third points sideways. The rotational movements are called *roll, yaw* and *pitch*, respectively. Linear movements along these axes are called *surge, heave* and *sway*, respectively. Now, normal unconstrained motion involves 6 DOF, but if a motion platform only possesses 3 DOF, people sensitive to motion sickness are the first to notice the missing DOF. For example, a low-cost motion platform may be constrained to roll, pitch, and heave: but are used with simulator ride experiences containing all 6 DOF. Thus during the ride our vestibular system detects roll, pitch, and heave; our eyes detect roll, pitch, yaw, surge, heave, and sway, and the stomach reacts accordingly! The conflict between equilibrium signals provided by the vestibular system and the motion cues from the visual system are thought to be the cause of such motion sickness.

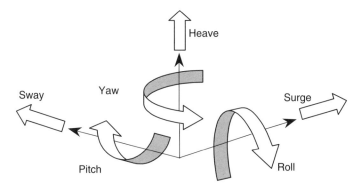

Figure 4.6   A 6-DOF axial system.

Fortunately, not everyone suffers from motion sickness, but one cannot ignore the effect it has, and it is possible to minimize its effects with a little thought.

4.7 Summary

Even from this brief overview of human factors it is obvious that it is going to be extremely difficult to find a range of technologies that will mimic the senses of sight, sound, touch, and balance. But if we remember that the objective of VR is not to replicate our experience of the real world, but to make things as realistic and useful as possible, then solutions are within our grasp.

Engineers will not want to tap a virtual component with a virtual hammer to hear what sound it makes, neither will they want to lift up a virtual car engine to estimate its weight. Similarly it will not be necessary to feel the temperature of a virtual tractor when its engine is running, nor will it be necessary to simulate heat haze, exhaust fumes, and the vibrations and rattles made by virtual components.

If VR is to be used by a wide community of people it must:

- be easy to use;
- accommodate a wide variety of human sizes;
- not cause fatigue;
- not induce nausea;
- not require long periods of adaptation.

It is very easy to upset our sensory systems. Even wearing reading glasses that are optically too strong can cause fatigue and disturb our sense of balance; therefore, great care is needed in the design of HMDs.

Although sound is a useful complementary cue, it does not have to be as accurate as the visual channel. Simple, relevant sounds relayed over headphones are often more than adequate to introduce an added sense of realism for most projects. The same is probably true for touch and haptic forces. Yes, it would be nice to feel a virtual object when our fingertips first make contact, but there is no need for such sophistication if there is no real added value.

Perhaps the one sense that requires careful attention above all is equilibrium. It is quickly disturbed, especially by conflicting cues from the visual channel and vestibular system. And it is rather unfortunate that somewhere along the line, the stomach became hardwired within the sensory communication network!

The simulation industry has for many years been able to work within the human body's sensory envelope when designing training simulators; therefore it should not be too difficult for the VR community to devise equally compatible systems.

5
VR Hardware

5.1 Introduction

In this chapter I want to describe the hardware used in various virtual reality (VR) systems. Such hardware is evolving very fast, and rather than concentrate upon specific manufacturer's models, I will describe generic devices and their operational characteristics and refer to specific systems where appropriate. Those readers who wish to discover the technical details of commercially available systems can look at manufacturer's web sites listed in Appendix E.

Under this heading of hardware we will look at the computers, tracking technology, input devices, glasses, displays, and audio. It will not be an exhaustive list, but sufficient for the reader to appreciate the range of technologies available.

Before we start though, it is time to consolidate our ideas about three terms that have been introduced in previous chapters: refresh rate, update rate, and lag or latency. These terms are used in association with tracking systems, image generators (IGs), and entire VR systems.

5.1.1 Refresh Rate

Refresh rate is associated with some form of display device such as a television, computer monitor, or head-mounted display (HMD). It defines how often the screen is refreshed with an image – which may be the same image, or a new image. In television technology an image is composed of two parts called fields: one field consists of the odd rasters and another field consists of the even rasters. This is called interlacing. Figure 5.1 shows the two fields formed by a television cathode ray tube (CRT). The solid horizontal line is the raster where the image is being refreshed, and the diagonal dashed line represents the fly-back part where the beam is blanked and

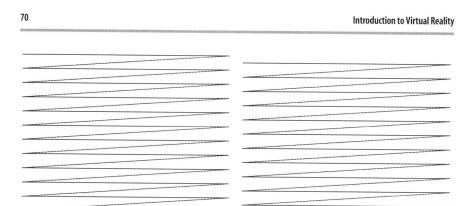

(a)   (b)

Figure 5.1   The two fields that make a video frame: (a) odd rasters and (b) even rasters.

Table 5.1 Field and frame rates for the USA and UK.		
	USA (NTSC)	UK (PAL)
Field rate (Hz)	60	50
Frame rate (Hz)	30	25

repositioned for the next raster. Interlacing the odd field followed by the even field keeps the image refreshed. For video technology there is a field and frame refresh rate, and Table 5.1 shows these speeds for the Phase Alternation Line (PAL) coding system of UK and the National Television System Committee (NTSC) coding system of USA. The reason for dividing an image into two parts is to minimize the frequency bandwidth of the broadcast signal, and to reduce flicker by maximizing the refresh rate.

A television receives its new images from the signals detected by its aerial, and as there are a specified number of fields transmitted, what all the television circuitry has to do is keep everything synchronized. However, a computer monitor has its image maintained inside a portion of memory that is updated whenever the computer is instructed. Today, most computer monitors are non-interlaced, and the entire frame is refreshed at a speed that causes minimum flicker, and is in the order of 72 Hz.

5.1.2 Update Rate

The update rate is the rate at which the *content* of the image is updated. For example, in television, a video camera samples a scene at the video rates shown in Table 5.1, which means that the update rate equals the refresh rate. But in a computer, the update rate is determined by the speed at which software is executed. For example, if a computer can only execute the renderer program at 10 Hz, there will only be 10 different images seen every second, but the monitor will still attempt to refresh the screen at its refresh rate. And say it takes exactly 0.5 s to render an image, and the

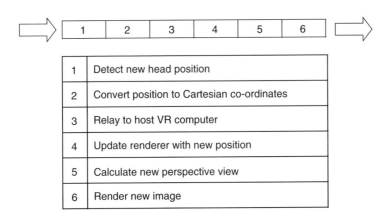

Figure 5.2 Pipeline of activities between head tracking and display of image.

refresh rate is 72 Hz; the monitor will display the first image 36 times and the second image 36 times.

5.1.3 Latency

Latency or lag is the time delay between an event occurring and its observation. In the context of television, the time between an event recorded by a camera and seen on a television screen is a very small fraction of a second. This is because the signals coming from a video camera pass through cables and electronic circuits at a speed approaching the speed of light (300,000 km/s). And when a television transmitter radiates these signals, they pass through space at the speed of light until intercepted by an aerial. Thus even if the signal has to travel 100 km, there is only a delay of 0.0003 s!

In computers anything can happen: I can touch a key, and a letter appears on the screen virtually instantaneously; but if the operating system suddenly decides to auto-save my file to hard disk, I might wait 4 or 5 s before the screen responds to keyboard activities. In such an environment the latency varies according to how busy the processor is.

In a VR system, latency can be the time that elapses between a tracking system detecting a new head position and the user seeing a corresponding image on the display. Figure 5.2 shows how the process of recording the position of the user's head to the display of a corresponding image can be visualized as a sequential pipeline of activities.

For simplicity, let us assume that all six activities are running at 50 Hz. This means that each activity in the pipeline is taking 0.02 s (1/50 s) to process a new piece of data. Therefore, the total latency is 6 × 0.02 which equals 0.12 s. Thus, it is the number of sequential stages that introduces latency.

The terms refresh rate, update rate, and latency will surface again in the following hardware descriptions.

5.2 Computers

Computers come in all shapes and sizes: from the humble personal computer (PC) to the massively parallel supercomputer used for simulating global weather patterns, or cosmological 'big bangs'. Today, however, virtually all computers are able to create pictures of some sort, and are therefore potential candidates as a VR platform. But, every computer has processing limitations, which ultimately dictates the complexity of three-dimensional (3D) images they can manipulate. We will now take a brief look at PCs, graphics workstations, supercomputers, and IGs.

5.2.1 PC

We saw in Chapter 3 that a VR application really stretches a computer to the very limit. In some instances it has to hold the 3D database, produce real-time, shaded, stereoscopic views of the virtual environment (VE), support audio, simulate animated sequences, support user interaction, and perhaps work collaboratively with other users. Such a range of tasks can easily exceed the operational envelope of many PCs, but if we are prepared to lower our expectations slightly, a PC is able to cope with many simple VEs.

Most PCs are fitted with some sort of graphics facility to support multimedia applications and the display of two-dimensional (2D) and 3D graphics. Although such PCs can display simple VEs, high-performance graphics cards are required to provide the real-time display of large databases. The specification of such cards includes parameters such as:

- a range of resolutions;
- large on-board texture memory;
- perspective correct texture mapping;
- sub-pixel and sub-texel positioning;
- texture morphing;
- Gouraud-modulated textures;
- video texture mapping;
- anti-aliasing;
- number of textured triangles rendered per second;
- sustained pixel fill rate;
- NTSC/PAL standards;
- per-pixel fog, smoke, and haze effects.

The resolution for most HMDs is in the order of 640h × 480v, whereas for monitors it is typically 1280h × 1024v.

Rendering speed is measured in terms of how many pixels can be written per second and/or millions of textured triangles per second, with most graphics cards currently exceeding a fill rate of 1 billion pixels/s and approaching 1 hundred-million triangles/s. However, one must be careful when comparing these specifications, as triangles are measured in different ways. To estimate the maximum rate at which the computer can update the viewing of the VE (the *update rate*) we divide the rendering speed by the number of displayed triangles. For example, if the rendering speed is 1 million triangles/s, and the VE contains 20,000 visible triangles, the maximum update rate is approximately 50 Hz, which is more than adequate for any VR application. But this is for a single view of the VE. If left and right views are required the performance will reduce to 25 Hz, which is still adequate.

In the field of computer games – which must be accepted as a form of VR – general-purpose PCs are becoming an important commercial platform. And publishers of computer games have already realized that they must supply games that run on PCs as well as the various game stations such as PS2. With the recent trend towards Windows NT/XP/etc., and clock speeds approaching 5 GHz, it is inevitable that PCs will become a major force in future VR systems. They already exist and enable users to configure a powerful VR system simply by plugging various boards to support VR peripherals such as HMDs, mice, and trackers. The advantage of this approach is that the PC still remains a PC, and can be used for all of the normal functions of word processing, spreadsheets, slide presentations, etc., as well as supporting VR when needed.

5.2.2 Graphics Workstation

Computer graphics workstations have always played an important role in supporting VR applications. Their cost varies considerably and they have always outperformed PCs, but today's PCs offer comparable performance at a reduced cost, and are vigorously challenging this position.

Computer graphics workstations operate within a UNIX/LINUX operating system, and although they may work with processor clock speeds that are comparable with PCs, it is their internal data channels and architecture that provide the added performance. The UNIX/LINUX operating system provides an ideal environment for developing software, and given the choice, programmers will often prefer a workstation rather than a PC to develop code, although a PC using LINUX provides an excellent compromise.

Graphics workstations are also specified in terms of their rendering speed, and although, they may provide extra performance, it is not inevitable that this will always be the case. Current 3D graphics cards have a fantastic performance, and the distinction between PCs and workstations is become increasingly blurred.

5.2.3 Supercomputer

Certain types of supercomputers generally manufactured by Silicon Graphics, Inc. are often used for high-end VR applications. Such machines are used because of the superior rendering speeds. The rendering process introduces environment and texture mapping and can even include shadows. They are used for the real-time display of very large VEs and in displays where three projectors create a panoramic image, or in a cave automatic virtual environment (CAVE). Apart from their rendering performance, their computational power can also be harnessed to support event simulation within the VE. But as one might expect, such performance has an associated higher price tag.

5.2.4 IG

Finally, IGs are specifically designed to produce real-time images, and are widely used throughout the simulation industry. One very important application is in civilian and military flight simulators.

Evans & Sutherland are world famous for their IGs and produced their first real-time line drawing system in 1968. Today, they produce a range of systems including their harmony PC-based product and the ESIG range of IGs. The ESIG-5500 IG offers an incredible range of features that are summarized below:

- Modes: day, dusk, night, infrared.
- Channels: eight per system and 64 viewport definitions.
- Anti-alisaing.
- Update rate: maximum 180 Hz, typically 15 or 60 Hz.
- Refresh rate: maximum 180 Hz, typically 50 or 60 Hz.
- Transport delay: 60 ms at 60 Hz.
- Resolution: expandable up to 2K × 2K pixels/video output.
- Displayed surfaces: expandable to over 550,000 polygons/s per channel processor.
- Displayed lights: expandable to over 24K per channel.
- Mission functions: collision detection, height above terrain, line-of-sight ranging, laser range finding.
- Directed lights: landing lights, steerable searchlight, headlights.
- Atmospheric effects: 3D clouds, smoke, fog, ground fog, haze, glare, scud, horizon glow, thunderstorm cell, lightning.
- Surface effects: Gouraud shading, self-luminous surfaces, continuous time of day, sun/moon.
- Texture: 8-, 16-, and 32-bit texels, contour texture, transparency, texture motion/ animation.

It is obvious from such a state-of-the-art specification that the simulation industry is well served, and demonstrates what can be achieved with today's technology (see Fig. 5.3).

5.3 Tracking

In recent years many technologies have emerged to capture the motion of humans. Some of this technology is used in computer animation and some for VR systems.

Figure 5.3 Typical scene from the E&S Harmony 2 IG. Image courtesy of Evans & Sutherland Corporation.

In computer animation character animation is particularly difficult, especially when a high level of realism is required, and although scripting and key-frame animation can obtain good results, motion capture is even better.

In VR, tracking technology is required to monitor the real-time position and orientation of the user's head and hand. In some applications the user's arm is required and in some instances the entire body. The technologies currently used in VR include mechanical, optical, ultrasonic, and magnetic, and Appendix C lists some popular systems.

Latency and the update rate are two important parameters associated with trackers, and out of the two it is the latter that is most important. The update rate determines the time taken between measuring a position and its availability to the VR software. If this becomes too high, say 100 ms, it makes interaction and navigation very tiresome.

5.3.1 Mechanical

A simple mechanical tracker can take the form of mechanical arm jointed at the shoulder, elbow, and wrist. When one end is fixed, the 3D position of the other end is readily calculated by measuring the joint angles using suitable transducers. The electromechanical nature of the device gives it high accuracy and low latency, but its active volume is restricted.

Mechanical trackers are very useful when integrated with a hand-held display. Fakespace, Inc., in particular, has pioneered this form of technology with products such as their BOOM3C, BOOMHF, PUSH1280, PUSH640 and PINCH (see Fig. 5.4).

5.3.2 Optical

One popular form of motion capture employs infrared video cameras that record the movement of a person. Attached to the person is a collection of markers in the form of small balls fixed to critical joints. When the moving person is illuminated with infrared light the marker balls are readily detected within the video images. As the

Figure 5.4 Fakespace BOOM 3C. Image courtesy of Fakespace Corporation.

system depends on the line of sight, the orientation of the cameras must be such to ensure that the markers are always visible. The positions of the markers within the video images are identified by host software and triangulated to compute their 3D position in space. If the 3D points are stored as a file, they can be used at some later date to animate the joints of a computer-animated character to great effect. If, however, the 3D points are input to a real-time computer system they can be used to control some virtual character.

5.3.3 Ultrasonic

As the name suggests, ultrasonic trackers employ ultrasonic sound to locate the position of the user's head. They are generally used for *fish-tank VR*, where a user is seated in front of a monitor screen, but gets the impression of seeing a volume of space in the form of a fish tank inside the monitor. The ultrasonic tracker is placed on top of the monitor and records the user's head movements. The signal is sent to the display software, which in turn updates the image with an appropriate perspective view. The advantages are that it is simple, effective, accurate, and low cost; but it is restricted to working within a small volume, it is sensitive to temperature, and depends on the line of sight.

5.3.4 Electromagnetic

Electromagnetic tracking technology is very popular and is used to monitor the position and orientation of the user's head and hand. The system employs a device called

Figure 5.5 The Polhemus Fastrak tracker. Image courtesy of Polhemus.

Figure 5.6 The Polhemus Ultratrak Pro. Image courtesy of Polhemus.

a *source* that emits an electromagnetic field, and a *sensor* that detects the radiated field. The source, which can be no bigger than a 2-in. cube can be placed on a table or fixed to a ceiling. The sensor is even smaller and is readily attached to an HMD or fitted within a 3D mouse.

When the sensor is moved about in space it detects different magnetic fields that encode its position and orientation. When the decoded signals are relayed back to the host VR computer, they modify the displayed view or the position of a virtual 3D cursor. The latency of these systems is very low – often less than 10 ms – but another parameter to watch for is the update rate, as this determines the number of samples returned to the host computer.

As electromagnetic fields are used, there are no line-of-sight restrictions, however the active volume is restricted to a few cubic metres, and large metallic objects readily disturb the fields.

Figures 5.5 and 5.6 show the Polhemus *Fastrak* and the *Ultratrak Pro* trackers, respectively.

5.3.5 Active Infrared

A recent development in real-time tracking comes from Hypervision, Ltd., who are based in the UK. Plate 10 shows their reactor system, which employs small infrared emitters placed at the user's joints. The user then moves inside a frame containing rows of infrared detectors, which detect and locate the spatial position of the emitters. By exploiting the characteristics of light propagation, triangulation is avoided, and within 20 ms or so, the system knows the precise position of any emitter. What is more, the system is self-aligning, and not affected when the user's body masks an emitter.

The reactor system is perfect for capturing motion data for computer animation projects, and because of its structure provides a perfect method to monitor the movement of someone inside a CAVE.

5.3.6 Inertial

Inertial trackers use the Earth's gravitational or magnetic field to measure orientation, and as they cannot currently determine position, their application is limited in VR. See Hollands (1995) for a detailed survey.

5.4 Input Devices

The input devices normally associated with a VR system are the 3D mouse and glove. Other esoteric devices are being developed but only exist as research tools, and are therefore omitted from this *essential* overview.

5.4.1 3D Mouse

A 3D mouse is a hand-held device containing a tracker sensor and some buttons, and is used for navigating or picking objects within a VE. In navigation the orientation of the mouse can be used to control the forward speed, while the user's gaze direction dictates the direction of travel. For example, tilting the mouse forward could initiate a forward movement, and holding it vertical stops the motion. It would be foolish to arrange that leaning the mouse backward cause the user to fly backward; it would not only be very confusing but could easily induce motion sickness. Figure 2.6 shows Logitech's Spacemouse, Spacetec's Spaceball, and Virtual Presence's Spacestick.

5.4.2 Gloves

Hand gestures are an intuitive way of controlling a VR systems, and in early systems became very popular. Unfortunately, they were expensive and earned a reputation for unreliability.

A simple interactive glove is made from a lightweight material into which transducers are sewn to measure finger joint angles. The transducers can be strain gauges or fibre optics that change their physical characteristics when they are stretched. Most modern gloves are very accurate and are used to communicate hand gestures such as pointing and grasping to the host software, and in some cases return tactile signals to the user's hand.

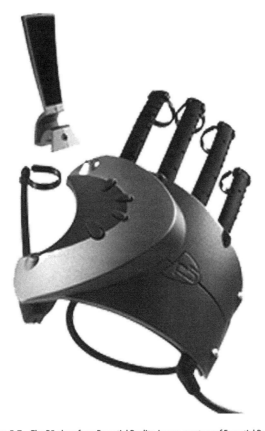

Figure 5.7 The P5 glove from Essential Reality. Image courtesy of Essential Reality.

While the glove monitors the orientation of the fingers, an extra tracker on the wrist monitors the position and orientation of the hand. Together, they enable a complete virtual hand to be animated within a VE.

Figure 2.9 shows the CyberGlove from Immersion Corporation. This has a tactile feedback option in the form of small vibro-tactile stimulators on each finger and the palm of the glove. These stimulators can create patterns of pulses and vibrations (125 Hz maximum) to confirm collisions with virtual objects.

Figure 5.7 shows the P5 glove developed by Essential Reality, which initially has been designed to work with specific computer games.

5.5 Output Devices

5.5.1 Force Feedback Sensors

Many modern cars tend to isolate the driver from forces that could be transmitted through the steering wheel. Such cars deprive the driver of valuable information relating to the stability of the car and the way it 'sits' on the road. Fortunately, it is still possible to buy cars that let the driver know exactly what the suspension is doing, and what is happening where the tires meet the road surface.

In civilian planes external forces are often fed back to the pilot through the flight controls, and are so important that they are replicated within a flight simulator. Thus when a pilot undertakes a banking manoeuvre or lands on a virtual runway, the host computer outputs appropriate signals that are turned into forces with the aid of electric motors. The overall effect is highly realistic.

The devices that return force information to a VR user are known as *haptic* devices as they provide some form of sensory feedback through the tactile senses. Thus it is possible to touch, weigh, and grasp virtual objects. However, we cannot feel, weigh, and grasp a virtual apple in the way we can a real apple – for the sensations from the virtual apple have to be communicated through some mechanical device. One way of appreciating the difference is to imagine an apple hidden inside a closed box. If we had a stick that could be inserted through a small aperture, we could feel the apple using the stick. We could sense its hard surface, its mass, and even its inertia when it rolled on the stick. It is these forces that can be fed back to a VR user through an appropriate 'force stick'.

If we had robotic technology in the form of a mechanical glove, it could be arranged that every finger joint could be activated by a small electric motor. Thus when we attempted to close our fingers together, appropriate signals could be sent to the motors to restrict our finger movement. When connected to a VE, it would be possible to grasp virtual objects and feel our fingers restrained from squashing the object.

If we wish to feel the weight of a virtual object our robot arm will have to apply forces that simulate the action of gravity. Thus, we will have to exert a force upward to overcome the effective weight of virtual object. One very effective haptic device is the PHANTOM Haptic Interface System from Sensable, Inc., and is shown in Fig. 5.8, Table 5.2, and Plate 17.

Force feedback is required in VR systems for molecular modelling systems, surgical training and training simulators for heavy machinery. And because each application has unique requirements, bespoke hardware is often required. However, a variety of joysticks are available that can provide forces to oppose a user's commands. Other more esoteric structures are still in research laboratories around the world, and we will have to wait some time before they surface as commercial products.

5.6 Glasses

Glasses with red and green filters are an excellent way of creating a 3D effect from a single overprinted red and green image (*anaglyph*). Similarly, glasses fitted with polarized filters can create stunning effects when looking at films projected through polarized light. Building upon the success of these simple techniques glasses have been developed to create 3D images when looking at a single monitor screen. An ideal solution however, should not involve glasses, but such technology is still being developed.

Figure 5.8   The PHANTOM 1.5/6 DOF. Image courtesy of Sensable, Inc.

Table 5.2   Technical characteristics of the Super Expanded Workspace PHANTOM.

Minimal position resolution	>1000 dpi	0.02 mm
Workspace	16 × 23 × 33 in	42 × 59 × 82 cm
Backdrive friction	0.75 oz	0.02 N
Maximum exertable force	4.9 lbf	22 N
Closed-loop stiffness	5.7 lbs/in	1 N/mm
Inertia (apparent mass at tip)	<0.34 lbm	<150 g
Footprint	8 × 8 in.	20 × 20 cm

5.6.1 Shutter Glasses

If we display alternately the left- and right-eye images of a VE on a monitor, the end result would be a blurred overlay. But if we could keep our left eye open when the left image was displayed, and similarly for the right eye with its image, we would obtain a 3D effect. This is impossible unaided because the images are switching to fast. However, we could get a pair of glasses to do the switching for us, and such glasses are called *shutter glasses*. The glasses operate by making the left- or right-hand lens opaque or transparent using liquid crystal technology, and they receive a synchroniz-

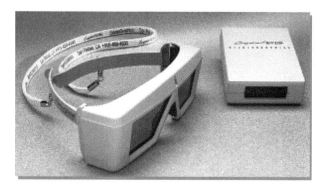

Figure 5.9   CrystalEyes. Image courtesy of Stereographics.

Table 5.3 Technical specification for the CrystalEyes shutter glasses.	
Transmittance	32% (typical)
Dynamic range	1000 : 1 min
Close time	0.2 ms (typical)
Open time	2.8 ms (typical)
Field rate	90–160 fields/s

ing signal from an infrared unit placed on top of the monitor. When the left image is displayed on the monitor a signal is sent to the glasses to shut the right-hand lens, and vice versa for the right image. The end result is a very realistic 3D effect that can be enhanced even further by including head tracking. There are however, two slight disadvantages: attenuation in brightness and ghosting. Liquid crystal display (LCD) filters are not perfect transmitters of light, and because they are unable to switch off completely, it is possible of one eye to see the other eye's image and cause ghosting.

CrystalEyes are the best-known shutter glasses for use in VR systems. They work with PCs, Macs, and workstations, and many computers come equipped with a jack point. Figure 5.9 shows the glasses, and a technical specification is shown in Table 5.3.

5.7 Displays

Display technology is central to any VR system, and to a certain extent is helping to classify the emerging configurations. And although real-time systems started with monitor-based computer graphics systems, it was the HMD that paved the way to what we now know as immersive VR. But since the emergence of HMDs other devices have appeared such as BOOM displays, CAVEs, virtual tables, and panoramic screens.

5.7.1 3D Screen

Stereographics manufacture a polarizing panel that transforms a projection system or computer monitor into a 3D display. Figure 5.10 shows the screen attached to a

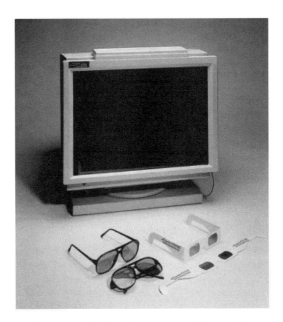

Figure 5.10 The ZScreen. Image courtesy of Stereographics.

monitor. The ZScreen operates somewhat like shutter glasses: when a left image is displayed on the monitor the image is polarized, say horizontally, and when the right image is displayed the polarization is vertical. Now if the viewer is wearing a pair of polarized glasses, their left and right eyes will see a sequence of corresponding left and right views of a scene.

The ZScreen has proved very useful for visualizing a wide variety of data sets, and because it is the screen that is active, the user simply dons a pair of passive polarized glasses.

5.7.2 HMD

HMDs possess a variety of characteristics such as *contrast ratio, luminance, field of view (FOV), exit pupil, eye relief,* and *overlap*. The contrast ratio is the ratio of the peak luminance to the background luminance, and a value of 100:1 is typical. Luminance is a measure of a screen's brightness, and ideally should exceed 1000 cd/m^2. The FOV is a measure of the horizontal and vertical visual range of the optical system, and ideally should approach that of the human visual system. In general though, most HMDs may only provide about 60° FOV for each eye. The exit pupil is the distance the eye can deviate from the optical centre of the display before the image disappears. This is in the order of 1.2 cm. Eye relief is a measure of the distance between the HMDs optical system and the user's face, and is in the order of 2 cm. And finally, overlap is a measure of the image overlap to create a stereoscopic image.

A typical HMD will contain two LCD elements viewed through infinity optics – that is to say they are collimated to infinity. The resolution is typically 640h × 480v pixels, and because one is so close to the elements, it is quite normal to discern the structure

Figure 5.11   The Virtual Research V8 HMD. Image courtesy of Virtual Research.

Figure 5.12   The Virtual Research V8 Binoculars. Image courtesy of Virtual Research.

of the pixels. No doubt, as display technology improves, we will have access to higher resolutions without higher costs. It should be noted that CRT-based HMDs do not suffer from this problem.

The horizontal FOV for each eye is in the order of 60°, while the vertical FOV is 45°, and for the user to perceive a stereoscopic effect there must be some overlap between the left- and right-hand images. It must also be possible to control the focus of each eye and adjust the distance between the pupils (the inter-pupilary distance).

Virtual Research manufactures a range of display systems that include Cyclops, the V6 and V8 HMDs, and the V8 Binoculars. The V8 HMD is shown in Fig. 5.11, and the V8 Binoculars are shown in Fig. 5.12. The technical specification for the V8 HMD is shown in Table 5.4. Appendix B lists some commercially available HMDs.

5.7.3 BOOM

Fakespace, Inc. is particularly known for its high-quality BOOM displays. These are stereo-devices supported by a counterbalanced arm, and employ high-resolution

Table 5.4 Technical specification for the Virtual Research V8 HMD.

LCD size	1.3-in. diagonal active matrix
Resolution	640 × 480
Contrast ratio	200:1
FOV	60° diagonal
Interoccular range	52–74 mm (adjustable)
Eye relief	10–30 mm (adjustable)
Stereo/mono-image sources	Automatically detected
Audio	Sennheiser HD25 headphones
Weight	29 oz (821 g)
Power consumption	30 W
Cable length	13 ft (3.9 m)

CRT technology. The user, who could be standing or seated manoeuvres the BOOM display using side grips into some convenient view of the VE. As the BOOM is moved about, joint angles in the articulated arm are measured to enable the 3D position of the BOOM to be computed. As this can be undertaken in real time, the position is supplied to the host computer to fix the viewpoint of the VE.

5.7.4 Retinal Displays

The Human Interfaces Laboratory at the University of Washington is still developing a retinal display that directs laser light direct onto the eye's retina. To date an 800-line monochrome system has been constructed and work is underway to build a full-colour system that works at an even higher resolution (Tidwell *et al.*, 1995).

5.7.5 Panoramic Screen

Military and commercial flight simulators have employed domes and panoramic displays for many years. Today, they are playing an important role in large VR centres where a group of 12 people, or so, can share the same visual experience. The screen is spherical and can be in the form of a dome, with a large horizontal and vertical FOV, or a cut down version with a restricted vertical FOV. In either format, three or more projectors are needed to cover the wide area, and for each projector an IG channel is required to render that part of the view. One of the problems of using multiple projectors is maintaining a consistent image quality across the screen. This calls for stable projectors where image linearity, colour balance, and brightness are maintained. Image linearity is needed to ensure that when an object moves from one projected image to another it occurs without distortion and without jumping rasters.

An innovative approach to immersive displays is available from the Elumens Corporation in the form of their Visionstation system (Fig. 5.13). This is a 1.5-m diameter hemispherical screen coupled with a single projector. Both the size, and spherical nature of the screen enhance the user's sensation of immersion very effectively. A larger system is shown in Plate 18.

Figure 5.13 The Elumens Visionstation hemispherical screen. Image courtesy of Elumens Corporation.

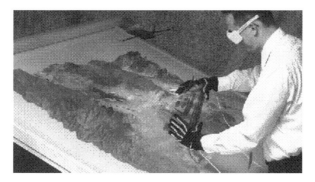

Figure 5.14 Fakespace's Immersive Workbench. Image courtesy of Fakespace.

5.7.6 Virtual Table

Virtual tables are an excellent idea and consist of a glass or plastic screen that forms a tabletop. Inside the table a projector displays an image of a VE onto the back of the screen with alternating left and right images. With the aid of shutter glasses and head tracking one obtains an excellent 3D view of the VE. The viewpoint is determined by the viewer and is strictly a one-person system; however, it is possible for two or more people to stand close together and share a common view. It has many uses especially for military, architectural, and medical applications.

Such systems were developed at the German National Computer Science and Mathematics Research Institute (GMD) and the Naval Research Laboratory and Stanford University. In 1996 Silicon Graphics, Inc. and Fakespace, Inc. announced their Immersive Workbench projected image display system at SIGGRAPH (see Fig. 5.14).

The resolution of the Workbench is 1600×1200 (monoscopic) and 1280×1024 (stereoscopic) at 120 Hz. The viewing area is 100 in. $\times$ 75 in. and can be adjusted from horizontal towards vertical. The Immersive Workbench can be applied to a wide range of applications including scale-model manipulation in design projects, medical visualization, military, and data visualization.

5.7.7 CAVE

In 1992, the University of Illinois at Chicago demonstrated their CAVE which has since developed into being a highly popular display system. A CAVE is constructed from a number of back-projection screens with external projectors projecting their images. Inside the CAVE a viewer is head tracked and wears shutter glasses, so that wherever he or she looks, a stereoscopic view is seen. The degree of immersion is very high and like the virtual table is strictly a one-person system; however, the room is normally large enough to allow other observers to share in the experience.

Figure 5.15 shows the projector layout for a four-sided CAVE. To reduce the volume of the system, the left, right, and rear projectors would have mirrors to reflect the

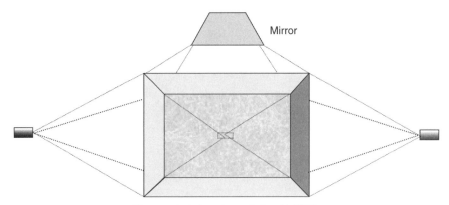

Figure 5.15   Projector layout of a four-sided CAVE.

Figure 5.16   Visualizing 3D medical data in a CAVE. Image courtesy of Pyramid Systems.

image onto the walls, as used in the ceiling projector. The size of a CAVE is normally a 3-m cube, but can be virtually any size. A high level of immersion can be achieved with three walls, but both the ceiling and floor can be used to totally immerse the viewer within a 3D VE.

As magnetic tracking systems are generally used to monitor the viewer's head, the CAVEs framework must be constructed from a non-metallic material, such as wood.

Pyramid Systems, Inc. manufacture a wide variety of CAVEs, and Fig. 5.16 illustrates one of their systems being used to visualize the structure of the human brain.

5.7.8 Augmented Reality

Augmented reality describes a VR system where computer-generated imagery is over-laid upon a normal view of the world. An HMD allows the wearer to see through a visor, and with the aid of special optical elements, a transparent computer image is

Colour Plates

Plate 1   Ray-traced front suspension of a Ford Fiesta. Image courtesy of ART VPS, Burrows of Essex, and the Ford Motor Company.

Plate 2   Ray-traced power train for a Ford Fiesta. Image courtesy of ART VPS, Burrows Essex, and the Ford Motor Company.

Plate 3 Ray-traced cutaway view of a Dyson washing machine. Image courtesy of ART VPS and Dyson Appliances.

Plate 4 A vizualization of an interior created by the LightWorks rendering system. Image courtesy of LightWorks Design.

Plate 5 Ray-traced view of a restaurant buffet area. Image courtesy of ART VPS and HOK Inc./Church of Scientology.

Plate 6 Ray-traced view of a restaurant. Image courtesy of ART VPS and HOK Inc./Church of Scientology.

Plate 7 Ray-traced interior view of an aircraft. Image courtesy of ART VPS and Bombadier Aerospace Inc.

Plate 8 Ray-traced interior view of an aircraft. Image courtesy of ART VPS and Bombadier Aerospace Inc.

Plate 9 Simulated boat and sea state using Softimage XSI. Image courtesy of Peter Hardie.

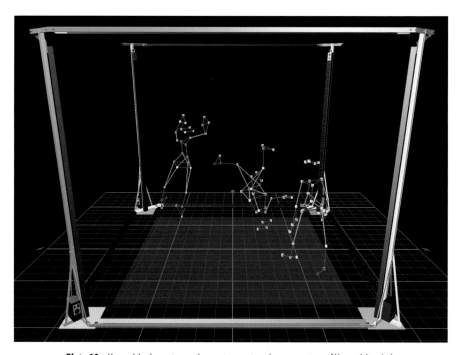

Plate 10 Hypervision's reactor motion capture system. Image courtesy of Hypervision, Ltd.

Plate 11 Internal view of a Viper. Image courtesy of James Hans.

Plate 12 External view of a Viper. Image courtesy of James Hans.

Plate 13 Radiosity view of the Tate Gallery created using the LightWorks rendering system. Image courtesy of LightWork Design.

Plate 14 Radiosity view of a kitchen created using the LightWorks rendering system. Image courtesy of LightWork Design.

Plate 15 A 360° view of a car interior for an environment map. Image courtesy of Jerome Dewhurst www. photographica.co.uk

Plate 16 A 360° view of a lounge for an environment map. Image courtesy of Jerome Dewhurst www. photographica.co.uk

Plate 17 The PHANTOM Desktop. Image courtesy of Sensable, Inc.

Plate 18 Visualization of the Elumens VisionStation. Image courtesy of Elumens Corporation.

Plate 19 Fractal-based 3D scene created by Blueberry3D. Image courtesy of Blueberry3D.

Plate 20 Fractal-based 3D scene created by Blueberry3D. Image courtesy of Blueberry3D.

Plate 21 Fractal-based 3D scene created by Blueberry3D. Image courtesy of Blueberry3D.

Plate 22 Fractal-based 3D scene created by Blueberry3D. Image courtesy of Blueberry3D.

Plate 23 DI-Guy 3D models positioned in a Blueberry3D fractal scene. Image courtesy of Boston Dynamics and Blueberry3D.

Plate 24 DI-Guy 3D models positioned in a Blueberry3D fractal scene. Image courtesy of Boston Dynamics and Blueberry3D.

Plate 25 VE for a hang glider simulator. Image courtesy of Dreamality Technologies.

Plate 26 VE used for a light aircraft simulator. Image courtesy of Dreamality Technologies.

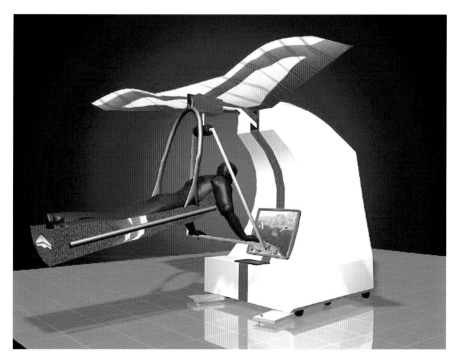

Plate 27 Hang glider simulator. Image courtesy of Dreamality Technologies.

Plate 28 The Sky Explorer simulator manufactured by Dreamality Technologies. Image courtesy of Dreamality Technologies.

Plate 29 Enhanced image from a real-time VR visualization of an interior. Image courtesy of the VR Centre at Teesside University.

Plate 30 An image from a real-time VR visualization of an urban development. Image courtesy of the VR Centre at Teesside University.

Figure 5.17 The Kaiser Sim Eye. Image courtesy of Kaiser Electro-Optics, Inc.

also seen. It requires accurate tracking technology to ensure that the two scenes are accurately aligned.

An augmented reality system (Fig. 5.17) could be used to train personnel to undertake a complex task. For example, to aid a worker in producing a complex wiring loom, an augmented display could be used to prompt the person with the layout for each wire. While individual wires are being laid over a template, the worker sees in the display the physical path to follow.

Although such displays have been widely used by military fighter pilots, they are still being developed for commercial applications.

5.8 Audio

Although audio is important to some VR applications, not too much emphasis is given to its implementation. Sounds of engines, radios, ticking clocks, virtual telephones, mechanical machinery, and other ambient sounds are easily played back over headphones incorporated into an HMD. However, where accurate sound positioning is required various digital signal processing (DSP) audio systems are available that exploit the HRTFs described in Chapter 4.

One company specializing in DSP audio systems is Lake DSP Pty. Ltd. who manufactures the Huron and CP4 systems. At the heart of both systems are DSP chips and some very clever software. For example, to simulate the acoustic properties of a virtual room, Lake's acoustic modelling software computes its *impulse response*, to capture the 3D acoustic properties of the room. This impulse response is then used to modify the frequency and phase response of any audio signal. This process is called *convolving*, and requires very high-speed computing techniques, hence the use of DSPs.

5.9 Summary

At the heart of any VR system is a computer that ultimately dictates the operational envelope of the system. Its role is simple. It has to provide a real-time environment for the software coordinating the various input/output devices, as well as the standard data storage and housekeeping facilities. For some applications an ordinary PC is more than adequate to provide a cost-effective solution, but for others a workstation or supercomputer is the only option.

When connecting any peripheral to a computer one requires software to manage the interface, and it may even be necessary to incorporate an extra processing board to look after specific tasks. Some companies even provide an extra unit to integrate an HMD, tracker, and 3D mouse.

As soon as one moves away from desktop VR, one enters a sector where specialist knowledge is required to configure hardware and integrate the software. Real-time computer systems are complex and one should not underestimate the level of expertise required to install, support, and repair them.

6
VR Software

6.1 Introduction

In the previous chapter we have looked at the various hardware elements associated with virtual reality (VR) systems, which included head-mounted displays (HMDs), mice, trackers, gloves, projectors, shutter glasses, and host computers. Software is now required to integrate these into a coherent system that will enable a user to navigate and interact with a virtual environment (VE). This is no mean task, because like all computer graphics applications, the software is application specific. For instance, a computer-aided design (CAD) system requires specific software tools and an appropriate interface to support the tasks required for two-dimensional (2D) and three-dimensional (3D) engineering designs. Similarly, a 3D computer animation system requires special tools for the modelling, animation, and rendering everything from dinosaurs to the *Titanic*. However, even though CAD and computer animation are both concerned with 3D objects, their requirements are totally different, and has resulted in many individual commercial software systems supporting both areas.

VR is also concerned with 3D objects, and although a CAD or computer animation system can be used to create a VE, they cannot be used to support the tasks of navigation and interaction. Special software is required to support navigation and interaction as well as collision detection, audio, visual level of detail (LOD), animation, simulation, etc.

By now you would have realized that VR systems can be configured in many ways and applied to dozens of different applications. At one end of the spectrum it is possible to create highly interactive 3D web sites that can be downloaded and manipulated on a personal computer (PC), and at the other end of the spectrum one can have immersive systems running on supercomputers. Although these two types of systems have different software systems, some of their requirements are common. Such software is readily available and I will try to provide a generic overview of the essential features required, and then give an overview of some commercial systems.

6.2 VR Software Features

6.2.1 Importing Models

It is pointless for any VR system to provide extensive software tools to model 3D objects or VEs – this is a complex task and many commercial modelling systems are available such as MultiGen, AutoCAD, Unigraphics II, CADDS5, Pro/Engineer, CATIA, 3D Studio MAX, MAYA, Lightwave, etc. However, a VR system *must* provide a mechanism for importing models from different systems – these are called *filters*.

As one might have expected, every modelling software system stores 3D information in a unique way. Furthermore, every VR system has its own internal file structure, which makes communication between different VR systems quite difficult. However, in spite of these problems, filters are available and models can be imported with minor difficulties. The sorts of problems that arise when importing models include the following:

- The CAD description may not be in a polygonal format. It could be surface patches or non-uniform rational B-splines (NURBs), or constructive solid geometry (CSG).
- The model may contain too many polygons.
- The model may contain polygons where as the VR system supports triangles.
- The vertex sequence of polygons may be different to that used in the VR system.
- The vertex sequence of polygons may not be consistent.
- The model may include duplicate polygons.
- The strategy for handling texture maps may be different.

There are many more such problems that have to be resolved by the filtering software.

6.2.2 Libraries

Most VR software systems provide a 3D library of some sort; this may be in the form of a collection of simple primitives such as polygons, boxes, spheres, cones, pyramids, etc., that can be assembled to create equally primitive VEs. Likewise, other libraries provide complete VEs in the form of office and home furniture, everyday objects, and complete rooms and offices. These are useful as they provide a starting point to become accustomed with working with a VE.

6.2.3 LOD

LOD is a system feature for optimizing the amount of detail rendered in a scene. For example, a model of a virtual house will require a lot of detail when viewed close to: it will include windows, doors, a chimney, gutters, and even individual tiles and bricks. If we go inside the house we could find internal walls, doors, stairs, furniture, and every type of fixture and fitting. However, if we look at the house from a distance of 500 m, individual tiles and bricks will appear very small, and we will certainly not be able to discern any internal contents through the windows. If we move even further away, some of the external features will disappear completely. Obviously, it would be a waste of time to render the same virtual model at these different distances. What is required is different models with appropriate LOD. A model viewed close up will contain fine levels of geometric detail, but when viewed at a great distance another model is substituted with corresponding lower LOD.

An LOD strategy requires copies of important models to be built that will be rendered at user-defined distances. These are stored together in the VE database, and the relevant model is rendered at the appropriate distance. This takes up extra disk space and memory at run time, but the rendering time saved makes it worthwhile.

One of the drawbacks of the technique is that it can be obvious when a model substitution is made. At one moment we see a view of a house, for example, with a particular LOD, and then all of a sudden a new one is substituted. The human visual system is particularly efficient at noticing such changes. However, the impact of the substitution can be minimized by fading out one view of the model and fading in the second view over a given distance and time. But this does require the renderer to handle transparency.

Another form of LOD control can be used when very large databases are manipulated, and cannot be rendered in real time. When the view is stationary the user sees the highest LOD possible. But as soon as the user navigates through the database the LOD switches to an appropriate level that permits a specific update rate to be maintained. When navigation stops, the database returns to its highest LOD.

Very powerful automatic software tools are available to create the alternative LODs of the database, and are generally prepared off line. This LOD strategy is particularly useful when manipulating very large CAD files.

6.2.4 Object Scaling, Rotating, and Translating

Some VR models may be nothing more than an imported CAD model, and will require very little manipulation. On the other hand, some VEs may require careful construction from several dozen individual elements. In the case of a house, the internal and external walls, windows, chimney, and roof will probably be modelled as one unit. Other features, such as doors, shelves, stairs, lights, work surfaces, cupboards, etc., will be modelled and installed individually.

To begin with, everything must share a common scale. Remember that a virtual house does not have to have coordinates that match a real house; coordinates do not have any physical units – they are pure numeric quantities. Maintaining a common scale is very easy – one simply multiplies or divides the object's coordinates by an appropriate number. In the jargon of computer graphics, this operation is called a *scaling transform*.

An object may have to be rotated before it is finally positioned, and various tools must be available to rotate specified angles about different axes. For instance, a ladder may have been modelled in a vertical position, but its place in the VE is leaning against a wall. Similarly, a door may be modelled facing the front of the house, and will have to be rotated by appropriate angles if it is to used in all of the rooms. Object rotation is achieved by a *rotation transform*.

Finally, once an object has been scaled and rotated, it has to be located within the VE using a *translation transform*. The use of these three transforms is a common procedure in VR software but the user rarely has to use them directly. Object scaling, rotating, and translating are normally effected through a graphics user interface (GUI) which makes life very easy. Figure 6.1 illustrates what happens to a box when it is subjected to a scale, translate, and rotate transforms.

But if VR is so good at interacting with 3D worlds, why not use a VR system to build a VE? Well, this can be done using MultiGen's Creator product.

6.2.5 Constraints

As we have already discovered, certain virtual objects require constraining to make them behave like their real-world counterparts. For example, a door requires to be constrained by its hinges and frame; a draw needs to slide in and out; the side windows of a car have to move up and down; a light switch must turn on and off, and a tap must turn clockwise and anti-clockwise. Such constraint information requires specifying and stored within the VE database. Thus when a VR user interacts with these objects, the database determines the limits of travel and prevents inconsistent

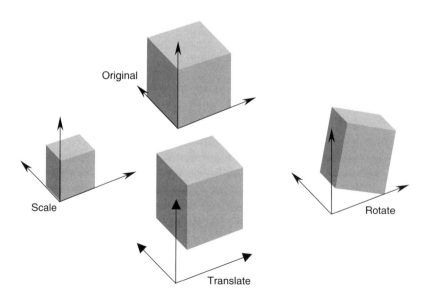

Figure 6.1   The effects of scaling, translating, and rotating an object.

manipulation. For instance, we would not want to approach a virtual door, request it to open, and find that it became attached to our hand! What we do want is for the door to open and be pushed to its physical limit without rotating through the supporting wall.

Other types of constraint include forcing objects to follow the floor height and preventing objects from intersecting other objects.

6.2.6 Articulated Features

VR is a very powerful tool for visualizing CAD models that often includes interconnecting elements. In the case of a car, for example, when one turns a real steering wheel, the front wheels turn accordingly; but one could not expect this to happen at a virtual level without a lot of work. It just so happens that such articulated features can be incorporated by identifying linked elements in a virtual object and forcing them to move whenever other elements move. Thus a VR user could use the controls of a virtual earth-moving vehicle to operate its hydraulically controlled digger. Such a facility is very useful for exploring the operational envelope of a piece of machinery and evaluating all sorts of ergonomic issues.

6.2.7 Animation

We have seen that it is possible to simulate the physical connectivity between various elements, which requires some pre-processing of the database and extra processing at run-time. However, it is not always necessary to simulate movements with such accuracy, and one can introduce simple animation to create a variety of animated behaviours. In flight simulation, animated models are used to mimic the behaviour of virtual ground crew assisting in bringing the virtual plane into a docking position. A sequence of models can be stored in the database in different positions, and can be played back in real time to create an animated effect. Although this requires extra effort to build the various models, it saves the processing time that would have been used to transform a single model into different positions.

Animation techniques can be used to simulate doors opening, water flowing, wheels rotating, weather effects, explosions, etc. Even video clips can be introduced into a VE by playing back Moving Pictures Experts Group (MPEG) files as an animated texture map.

6.2.8 Collision Detection

We already know that collision detection provides a method for selecting objects within a VE. For example, when a hand-held 3D mouse is used to guide the virtual cursor inside a VE, the polygons associated with the cursor can be tested for collision against other objects. When a collision is detected, we can request that the object be associated with the cursor, which can be used to re-position the object. It is the real-time software environment that undertakes this task, and because collision detection can become very time consuming, especially when one complex object is compared with the VE, very efficient algorithms are essential.

In order to keep the VR system running as fast as possible collision detection must be kept to a minimum, but there are many occasions when it provides the only way of working. Thus a user will require to activate and deactivate this mode of working even when working immersively, which calls for appropriate interface tools.

6.2.9 Parallel Worlds

The rather imposing name of *parallel worlds* has been borrowed from the esoteric realms of cosmology, but in this context it simply means multiple databases. One can move from one world (VE database) to another by passing through a portal which is a doorway connecting to another VE. It is a convenient way of moving from the outside of a building into its inside without having to store one large database. When we are outside the building we cannot see its inside and vice versa. Whenever we pass through the portal the real-time software makes the necessary database substitution.

6.2.10 Light Sources

At some stage lights have to be positioned within the VE. This may be nothing more than setting an ambient level and one major light source. However, if the VE is representing a detailed interior model, and illumination levels are important, several lights will have to be positioned and adjusted to create the required visual effect.

Perhaps the most sophisticated lighting model is radiosity that simulates inter-reflections, colour bleeding, and soft shadows. Although there is no real-time solution at the moment, it is possible to compute these light levels off line and import them with the VE geometry. This creates highly realistic images with hardly any run-time over-head. As shadows and illumination are integral with the geometry, their values cannot be changed on line. Plate 13 shows excellent example of the radiosity technique.

6.2.11 Event Handling

Specific actions or animation are called *events* and require software to ensure they are correctly activated. Such events may take the form of doors opening automatically, an object reaching some destination, or the user moving into a special zone in the VE. For example, a virtual airplane attempting to land can have its landing gear automatically brought down when it reaches a set height above ground. Similarly, a VR user under-going training using a VE could wander into a 'dangerous' area and trigger an event in the form of an MPEG video clip. Whatever the reason, events can be activated to add that extra level of realism to a VE.

6.2.12 Audio

The VR software system must also control the playback of sound files associated with different objects and zones of a VE. Such sounds include ticking clocks, running engines, radios, telephones, machinery, human voices, and all sorts of ambient background noises. The sound volume, as heard by the VR user, can also be attenuated by the user's distance from the object. And a virtual radio, for example, could be switched on by touching its virtual on/off switch, or the engine noise of a mechanical digger could become louder every time it undertook a heavy task. Where required, the VR software must also support 3D sound systems.

6.2.13 Control Language

Just as a scripting language is needed in certain computer animation software systems, a similar control language is required to animate objects within a VE. For example, in a VR training exercise, when a user performs a certain action, a script is executed that undertakes a set task. This could be anything from opening a door to animate a bottling plant when a button is pushed. Either way, the script is interpreted by the real-time software to activate a preset animation.

6.2.14 Simulation

In the early days of VR the general public imagined that a virtual world was similar to the real world. How wrong they were! Very little happens inside a VE unless it is programmed, and if anything makes it happen, it is software.

Simulation software is complex and even the simplest of activities requires intense programming. Take, for example, object collision. When two real objects collide they obey Newtonian mechanics, which states that the combined momentum of the two objects remains constant before and after the impact. The momentum is the product of the object's mass and velocity. This is easy to compute mathematically, but when two irregular objects collide, their impact can give rise to an infinite number of collision scenarios that cannot be predicted. If accuracy is required the mathematical solution requires knowledge of the object's masses, linear velocities, angular velocities, moments of inertia, surface attributes, gravity, etc. But even then, it will be only possible to compute an approximate simulation if the answer is required in real time.

Therefore, unless there is a limited role for simulation within a typical VR system, substantial levels of processing power are available to execute the simulation programs. However, current software is attempting to simulate the effects of mass, gravitational forces, and forces due to interaction and collisions. With appropriate hardware such forces can be returned to the user via joysticks, gloves, and articulated arms.

6.2.15 Sensors

Anyone who has attempted to interface the simplest of devices to a computer will know of the technical challenge it presents. Not only is it necessary to have a detailed knowledge of the device, it is essential to have an intimate knowledge of the host operating system, whether it be Windows, Windows NT, UNIX, or LINUX. For devices such as printers, scanners, modems, fax machines, etc., there are some very efficient software tools for installing these in a matter of minutes, but the installation of HMDs, trackers, 3D mice, etc. requires careful handling.

VR software must include appropriate tools to interface the various sensors, and enable them to work within a real-time environment. Fortunately, this is an area that has been addressed by the VR community.

6.2.16 Stereo Viewing

Although HMDs have left and right screens to operate stereoscopically, it can be arranged for them to work monoscopically where both eyes see the same image. It is also necessary to adjust, at a software level, the distance between the user's virtual eyes (the inter-pupilary distance), and the degree of overlap between the left and right images. Some systems are also able to provide a parallel as well as a perspective projection of the VE.

6.2.17 Tracking

Tracking technology is a vital feature of any VR system and several systems are commercially available. Software support is required to enable the tracker's position to be located within the VE and adjusted to give the user a useful point of view.

6.2.18 Networking

Some VR systems can be networked together so that two distant users can share a common VE and interact collaboratively. Under such conditions there has to be a fast exchange of information between the computers.

Let us examine the case of two users: User A and User B who have the same VE installed in their computers. User A will want to see User B in his or her HMD, and vice versa, therefore the position of the two users must be exchanged. This enables each host computer to display a 3D mannequin of the other user. Such a mannequin is called an *avatar*. Each user's hand position must also be exchanged so that the avatar's arm and hand can be animated. Finally, the name of the object selected, together with its position and orientation must be exchanged, so that each computer can display the final scene.

By exchanging this minimal level of data over a fast communication network, two users can see each other at a virtual level and interact with a single object. However, only one user can have control of an object at any one time, but if each user takes it in turns, software will look after the transfer of control.

6.3 Web-Based VR

6.3.1 Introduction to VRML

Users of the World Wide Web (WWW) will be aware of its ability to distribute text and images across the network, but in recent years great strides have been made in implementing a strategy for distributing 3D worlds. The hyper-text markup language (HTML) has become the *de facto* standard for describing documents with hyperlinks, and a similar language was required for supporting interactive simulation within the WWW. The virtual reality modelling language (VRML) is the result – although it initially started its life as the VRML.

In 1994 the first *WWW Conference* was held in Geneva, Switzerland, and Tim Berners-Lee and Dave Raggett led a group to discuss the requirements of a 3D graphical language. It had to be platform independent, extensible and work over low-bandwidth networks. It was also decided that the first version of VRML would not support interactive behaviours – this would have to wait for a later revision.

The idea of attempting to implement 3D graphics over the Internet still seems a strange idea, especially when the system response of the web can appear as though the whole world is connected, to one being the only user! But VRML has proved to be successful.

Fortunately, it was not necessary to start from scratch, as it was possible to call upon an extensive history of 3D computer graphics. And in the end, Silicon Graphics' Open Inventor American Standard Code for Information Interchange (ASCII) file format became the basis of VRML as it already supported polygonal objects, lighting, materials, rendering, and texture mapping.

6.3.2 VRML Browsers

A VRML file stores a description of a 3D world in the form of graphic primitives, their colour and texture, and how they are to be viewed by a virtual camera. It is also possible to subject the objects to the transforms: scale, translate, and rotate. When such a file is stored on the web, any user can download it and store it on their computer. Then with the aid of a suitable browser it is possible to convert the ASCII file into a 3D image. But as the browser is equipped with tools to rotate, pan, and track, one can navigate a 3D model in real time. It is the speed of the host computer that determines the processing speed, rather than the communication network.

6.3.3 VRML 1.0 Specification

Although this is not the place to give a complete overview of VRML, it is worth exploring some of its features in order to appreciate its potential. A full specification is located at http://www.vrml.org/VRML1.0/vrml10c.html.

6.3.4 Nodes

Nodes are the building blocks for creating 3D computer graphics, and include cubes, spheres, cones, cylinders, etc.; transformations (scale, translate, and rotate), colours, textures, viewing perspective, etc. The nodes are organized into a specific sequence called a *scene graph* such that when they are traversed, their order determines the sequence the 3D world is created.

A node can also influence other nodes further along the scene graph. For example, a colour node can be declared such that any following object nodes can be given the same colour. Similarly, a scaling transform node could be used to collectively translate a number of object nodes. In order to cancel the influence of these nodes a *separator node* is used to partition the scene graph into organized structures. A node has the following characteristics:

- Object type—cube, sphere, texture map, transform, viewer orientation, etc.
- Node parameters—height, radius, width, depth, red, green, blue, x, y, z, etc.
- Name of node—an arbitrary name to allow multiple referencing.
- Child nodes—nodes that belong to a larger hierarchy.

6.3.5 VRML File Format

The first line of a VRML 2.0 file must contain the characters '#VRML V2.0'. Subsequent lines refer to the nodes that comprise the scene graph. As internal documentation is a *must* for all computer languages, VRML employs the '#' symbol to delineate the start of a comment, and is terminated by a new line.

The rest of the file comprise a number of statements about the position of the camera, texture maps, the type of object, the object's position, etc. For example, the geometry for a cube could be defined as:

Geometry Cube {height 4 width 3 depth 2}

and a sphere as:

Geometry Sphere {radius 2}

The default position for a perspective camera is $(x = 0, y = 0, z = 1)$ but this can be overridden by the following command:

PerspectiveCamera {position 0 1 20}

Every other command has its own list of parameters. A complete VRML 1.0 program is shown in Appendix D.

The first version of VRML was issued over 10 years ago, and since then version 2.0 has surfaced with many more extras. In December 1997, VRML 97 replaced VRML 2.0 and was formally released as International Standard ISO/IEC 14772. If you really want to find out more about VRML 2.0, take a look at Jed Hartman and Josie Wernecke's book *The VRML 2.0 Handbook* (1996).

The following VRML program produces the image in Fig. 6.2. But by using the interactive tools in the browser one can immediately rotate the scene to obtain the view shown in Fig. 6.3.

#VRML V2.0 utf8
Background {skyColor 1.0 1.0 1.0}
Group {
 children [
  # Box shape

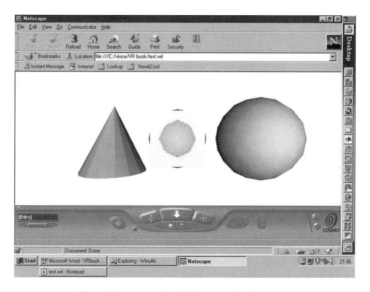

Figure 6.2   Output of the VRML program described in text.

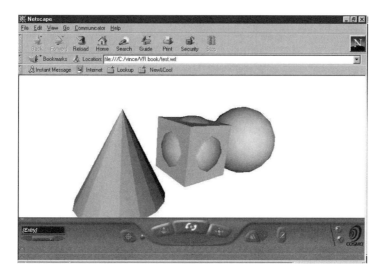

Figure 6.3   Rotated view of VRML model.

```
Shape {
  appearance Appearance {
    material Material {
      diffuseColor 1.0 1.0 0.0}
  }
  geometry Box { size 3.0 3.0 3.0}
  }
```

```
# Sphere shape
Shape {
  appearance Appearance {
    material Material {
      diffuseColor 0.0 1.0 0.0}
}
geometry Sphere {radius 1.8}
}
# Right Sphere
 Transform { translation 5.0 0.0 0.0
   children [
   Shape { appearance Appearance {
     material Material {
       diffuseColor 0.9 0.9 1.0}
   }
     geometry Sphere {radius 2.5}
   }
   ]
 }
# Left Sphere
 Transform { translation -4.0 0.0 0.0
   children [
   Shape {
     appearance Appearance {
       material Material {
         diffuseColor 0.8 0.8 0.5}
   }
   geometry Cone { bottomRadius 2.0 height 4.0
                 side TRUE bottom TRUE}
  }
  ]
 }
 ]
}
```

As one can see, even small programs are very verbose, and large programs require great care to assemble. Fortunately, a variety of interactive software tools are available to ease the design of VRML worlds.

6.4 Division's dVISE

6.4.1 Overview of dVISE

Division Ltd. pioneered the design of VR software to meet the demanding needs of the industrial sector. Today, they have become part of Parametric Technology Corporation.

Their dVISE system was the result of many years' R&D effort and collaborative industrial projects that gave VR a true professional image.

dVISE allows a designer to create a virtual representation of a product (i.e. a virtual product) based on the engineering data from a CAD database. It allows the designer to add audio, visual, and behavioural characteristics (such as animation, movement constraints, and collision properties) to this representation, so that dVISE can model the interaction of the product's component parts and the interaction of the product with human operators.

dVISE is a modular product with each module carefully targeting a specific function. All modules support SGI, HP, and Sun UNIX platforms in addition to PCs running Windows NT. A summary of all the modules is included in the following sub-sections and listed in order of increasing functionality.

All dVISE modules support interactive navigation through the virtual product using a normal desktop mouse and workstation monitor. Some modules support more advanced peripherals, such as 3D mice and stereo-HMDs. In addition, many modules include advanced navigation aids that allow users to fly to stored positions via an iconic GUI.

6.4.1.1 *dV/WebFly*

The dV/WebFly module allows virtual products to be published on the Internet and viewed using a freely available plug-in for commercial HTML browsers.

6.4.1.2 *dV/Player*

The dV/Player module is a high-performance visualization tool. It is designed for real-time navigation of very large assemblies and provides users with the capability to move assemblies, to view Landmarks (camera views), and to playback complex animations. This module includes a basic level of collision detection in which a bounding box represents each assembly.

Output from this module is displayed on a workstation, with support for CrystalEyes glasses for a pseudo-stereo-effect. Navigation is controlled by a conventional mouse, a Spaceball, or a Spacemouse.

6.4.1.3 *dV/Review*

The dV/Review module includes all the functionality of the dV/Player module, but also allows the user to create, edit, and view Landmarks and user Annotations (user notes), and to save these definitions to the file system as part of the virtual product's definition. The Virtual Product Manager is included in this module, and may be used to view and edit the assembly hierarchy (using a 2D graphical display), to selectively load or unload assemblies, and to send dVISE events to assemblies.

6.4.1.4 *dV/MockUp*

The dV/MockUp module includes all the functionality of the dV/Review module, plus fast polygonal collision detection, interference analysis, and extended Virtual Product Manager capabilities. The latter allows the user to edit the assembly structure, to define the animation properties of assemblies, to add user data into the assembly hierarchy, and to define the illumination of the virtual product.

The fast polygonal collision detection algorithms enable the user to study the interaction of complex assemblies in real time, and are ideally suited to the modelling of assembly/disassembly sequences. dV/MockUp and dV/Reality are the only modules that include this feature; other modules use fast-bounding box collision detection in which the collision boundaries of each assembly are modelled by a bounding box.

Users of dV/MockUp and dV/Reality may perform a product-wide interference analysis on the virtual product to check that assemblies do not interfere or overlap by more than a specified tolerance. The interference test may take the form of a single query or it may accommodate animated models via a continuous query and real-time display of results. In either case an interference report identifies assembly pairs that were found to collide and the points of collision. Optional links between the Interference Manager and the dVISE View allows the affected assemblies to be brought into view and highlighted.

The Virtual Product Manager functionality that is provided by dV/MockUp allows you to add assemblies into a hierarchy that defines a virtual product. You can associate user data with each assembly, perhaps recording the source of the data or general design notes. You can also edit and view the position, visual, and collision properties of the assemblies to specify their appearance and the way they respond to manipulation.

6.4.1.5 *dV/Reality*

The dV/Reality modules include all the capabilities of the dV/MockUp module, but extend the functionality of the Virtual Product Manager allowing you to design a fully functional model of your virtual product.

With the dV/Reality module you can specify the behaviour of your assemblies (i.e. how they respond to events) allowing you to model the way that your assemblies interact and respond to external influences. You can also constrain movements, and you can associate audio properties (such as musical or special effect sounds). You can also link assemblies to create assembly hierarchies that operate as a single entity; movement (or any other manipulation) of one entity will then affect those that are linked to it.

With the dV/Reality module you can define a fully functional virtual prototype that can be viewed by any of the dVISE modules.

6.4.2 Common Components

The dV/Geometry Tools component is an integral part of all the dV/Review, dV/MockUp, and dV/Reality modules. It includes stand-alone (off-line) converters and geometry processing tools for AutoDesk 3D Studio, DXF, Alias/Wavefront, and MultiGen formats. A number of options are also available for importing engineering data from specialist CAD environments. Supported formats include: Extended Data Services (EDS) Unigraphics, Pro/Engineer, Computervision CADDS and Optegra, IBM/Dassault CATIA, Bentley MicroStation and Intergraph (IGDS), Inventor, and IGES.

The dV/Collaboration component adds a networked multi-user capability to the dV/Review, dV/MockUp, and dV/Reality modules (and is available as an option for the dV/Player module). It also allows many users to view and interact with the virtual product concurrently and via a corporate local or wide area network.

6.4.3 Optional Components

- dV/Manikin   This option adds human modelling to all of the dVISE modules. It allows you to simulate the interaction between your virtual product and its human operators for applications such as ergonomics and component accessibility.
- dV/Immersion   This option adds a full immersive capability to all dVISE modules, and allows the use of 3D peripherals such as HMDs and 3D mice.
- dV/ITools   This option adds an immersive ToolBox, allowing you to control and define the VE immersively.
- dV/Developer   This option provides libraries and header files that let C programmers extend the capabilities of dVISE by defining new actions functions and new tools for an immersive ToolBox. You can also build upon Division's low-level interface to develop a custom application that replaces dVISE and more closely models the requirements of your virtual products.

6.4.4 A Virtual Product

Division defines a virtual product as one or more assemblies that are typically derived from CAD environments, and are converted into a form that is suitable for rendering by using the dVISE Geometry Tools.

During the conversion process the Geometry Tools extract from the CAD database all data that is relevant to interactive visualization. This includes the logical structure of assemblies (i.e. the sub-assembly hierarchy), colour and layer partitioning, assembly names, materials and textures, user-defined annotations, and, of course, the geometric data. After the conversion process the assemblies are represented by an assembly or product structure file that records the overall structure of the product, and by binary files that represent the geometric and material data.

6.4.4.1 *Virtual Device Interface Files*

The virtual device interface (VDI) file is the top-level representation of an assembly. It is a human readable (ASCII) scripting language for defining virtual products.

Within it you can define many assemblies and assembly hierarchies, their inter-dependencies, and their properties.

Each CAD conversion generates a single top-level VDI file representing an assembly or assembly hierarchy. Many conversions can be performed, possibly converting data from many different CAD environments, each resulting in a VDI file representation. dVISE allows the designer to assemble these VDI files into a product structure, and to assign physical properties that describe their interaction. The resulting product can be saved to a new VDI file that records the full product definition.

6.4.4.2 The dVISE Geometry Tools

The interface to the dVISE Geometry Tools is via a simple GUI. At the simplest level the tools will convert the geometric data into a form that is suitable for rendering (i.e. tessellation), and will also perform optimization, welding, reduction, and other geo-metric functions to maximize image quality and rendering performance.

Some high-end CAD environments also support active links with dVISE, and allow the export and conversion of data from within the CAD environment.

A key capability of the geometry tools is the ability to generate appropriate LODs. As a user moves around in the VE, dVISE optionally selects the most appropriate LOD to maximize image quality while retaining acceptable navigation performance. When the user stops moving the assemblies that are close to the viewpoint are switched to a high-resolution form that allows detailed analysis.

6.4.4.3 Interacting with the Virtual Product

You can view a virtual product on a conventional computer display within a dedicated window, called the dVISE View that can be resized and moved anywhere on the screen. You interact with the virtual product by using a conventional computer mouse, or a Spaceball or Spacemouse that provide a more intuitive way to manipulate the product in 3D. CrystalEyes glasses allow you to generate pseudo-stereo-displays from a work-station's monoscopic display.

For the greatest control you can use a stereo-HMD and a 3D mouse, which allow you to immerse yourself in a VE, and to move around and interact with the product in the most natural and productive way.

6.4.4.4 dVISE Navigation Aids

Some dVISE modules build upon the explicit directional controls of the hardware devices to provide a number of higher-level software controls. You access these con-trols via the Virtual Product Manager, which provides the user interface to all the high-level navigation and design capabilities of dVISE.

6.4.4.5 *Navigator View*

The Navigator View allows you to control your position in the VE by entering explicit directional or rotational movements into a GUI. This achieves more accurate positioning than the hardware controls, particularly for small incremental movements (see Fig. 6.4).

6.4.4.6 *Cameras, Flight Paths, and Landmarks*

A user can place cameras at interesting points in the assembly hierarchy to record important views of the assemblies. You can see these cameras represented as icons in the Assembly Manager, but the Landmark Browser provides a more intuitive (and more widely available) interface.

Flight paths build on the functionality of cameras to define an animated view of the virtual product. As with cameras there is an iconic representation of flight paths in the Assembly Manager, and links may be created from the Landmark Browser. When you activate a flight path or camera, your virtual body is flown smoothly along a prescribed path producing an animated view of the product.

6.4.4.7 *Annotations*

The Annotation Browser allows designers and reviewers to attach text messages (optionally with audio, visual, and behavioural properties) to a view, and to send the textual message of the annotation to other members of their team via a corporate e-mail system. The Annotation Browser collates the annotations and their responses into a graphical 2D display. When you review an annotation you can playback its

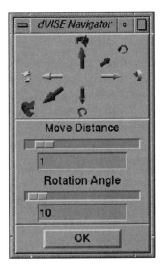

Figure 6.4 Navigator's controls. Image courtesy of Division Ltd.

associated voice recording and fly to the appropriate assemblies in the VE. The annotation may also define actions that bring the virtual product (or parts of it) to life.

6.4.4.8 *Events and Actions*

All dVISE modules support an event/action paradigm that allows complex behaviour
to be modelled. A designer can define the events that an assembly responds to and the
list of actions that are to be performed in response to those events. For example, an
assembly might move or play an audio track when it is touched. The events may be
issued by dVISE in response to physical stimuli (e.g. when you touch an assembly) but
more commonly they are issued by other assemblies to model their interaction.

6.4.4.9 *Multiple Users and Roles*

Most dVISE modules support a collaboration option that allows users to work
together within a VE. Users connect to dVISE from their own networked workstations, either via a local or wide area network, and are each represented in the VE by
an avatar (i.e. a user-defined geometric form). Changes that any one user makes to
the virtual product are immediately visible to all others users (including the definition of cameras, landmarks, and annotations). Users can also interact allowing them
to demonstrate recent changes by pointing to, and manipulating, assemblies.

Each instance of the Virtual Product Manager has an associated user context, which
by default represents the first user. This means that navigation controls will act on the
first body, and events sent from the Virtual Product Manager's Assembly Manager
will appear to originate from the first user. You can use the Virtual Product Manager's
User Browser to identify the other dVISE users, and to change the Virtual Product
Manager's user context. The Virtual Product Manager's navigation controls, for
example, will then manipulate another user's virtual body. Note however that by changing the Virtual Product Manager's user context you affect only the desktop interface
to dVISE; your input/output devices will still manipulate your own virtual body, and
you will retain your own perspective in the dVISE View.

dVISE also allows you to define *Roles* that define behaviour and immersive tools that
are tailored to specific user activities. You might want to define a *Trainer* and an
Engineer role, for example, which modify the user's behaviour and tools to mirror the
functions that might be performed by these two types of job. You can select a role
either when you start dVISE (via command line options) or you can select roles by
using the Virtual Product Manager's User Browser.

6.4.4.10 *The ToolBox*

For those users that elect to use immersive VR peripherals (such as HMDs and 3D
mice) most dVISE modules support an immersive ToolBox option – the dV/ITools
option. The ToolBox is a set of 3D tools that are accessible from within the VE. It provides an immersive interface to many design and navigation aids.

Design operations that you perform using the ToolBox are defined by explicit inter-action with assemblies. For example, you can select a constraint tool and an assembly in the environment and constrain the assembly by making natural 3D movements. You assign other attributes, such as lighting and audio, using similar interactive tools. You can animate an assembly by simply selecting it and pointing to positions that define the required motion.

You can configure the ToolBox to include the tools most appropriate to your own tasks. You can also define ToolBoxes for specific activities, and associate each with a user Role. The tools required for a review of your virtual product may differ from those of a design activity, for example, so you might want to define Reviewer and Designer roles.

6.4.4.11 *Using Templates and Libraries*

A designer can make templates of assemblies and then create many instances of them in the VE. With complex assemblies this can save a lot of work as the instances inherit all of their initial properties from the templates. Inheritance also makes it easier to build complex environments; the detail is encapsulated in the assembly template and you can treat the instance as a single component or building block.

For example, you might build up a robot arm from a number of components: a base, an arm, a wrist, and grippers. These components can be linked and their movements constrained to simulate the behaviour of a robot. If you make this a template then you can go on to create many instances of it. Each instance inherits all the properties of the template so the links and constraints are automatically set up.

The instances can be customized by selectively changing their inherited properties, or by adding new properties. Changes that are made to the template's properties affect all instances that inherit those properties; instances that have overridden the inherited properties with new properties are unaffected.

For example, all instances of the robot arm assembly might inherit a grey colour from the template, but you can selectively change some instances to another colour. If you subsequently decide that you want to change the grey colour, you can modify the template and implicitly change all grey instances.

6.4.4.12 *Libraries*

Libraries define a collection of assembly templates. A library can be defined as an integral component of a product's VDI file (in which case the templates are only applicable to one product) or it can be defined in a separate VDI file that contains only library definitions (in which case the templates are more widely available).

In addition to assembly templates the VDI file can also record key-frame templates, which define animation sequences. As animations can be complex (and time consuming to define) a designer might define a generic template that can be applied to any of the assemblies in the virtual product.

A second kind of library used by dVISE defines the materials (i.e. colours and textures) that can be applied to the surfaces of the assemblies. Materials are defined in basic material files (BMF), and are typically derived from the CAD environment when the assemblies are converted. Material files can also be created manually, and edited, as described in the *dVISE Geometry Tools User Guide*.

6.4.5 dVISE Summary

As one can see from this brief overview, dVISE has been designed to address the real problems encountered within the industrial sector. Division's knowledge of immersive and non-immersive VR systems is second to none, and dVISE is probably the most advanced VR product currently available.

6.5 Blueberry3D

Every now and then the world of computer graphics is taken aback by something truly outstanding. In recent years, this has included ray tracing, radiosity, and inverse kinematics, all, of which, have found their way into commercial animation systems. Another breakthrough belonging to this list is procedural fractal geometry, which has transformed the way we describe clouds and organic systems that exhibit self-similarity.

In the real world, everything is constructed from collections of molecules, which in turn are built from combinations of atoms. And as we get closer and closer to an object, we discover increasing levels of detail – apparently without end.

In a computer-generated world, we quickly discover the ultimate building block – the polygon – covered in some sort of texture. But just over 25 years ago fractals suddenly appeared on the stage of computer graphics through the work of Benoit Mandelbrot and others, and very quickly it was realized that fractals could be used to describe 3D terrain, clouds, trees, and other organic systems that exhibited some sort of self-similar structure (Peitgen and Saupe, 1988). For example, a tree can be considered as a trunk connected to a system of branches. The branches, in turn, can be considered as smaller trunks connected to collections of twigs. Even the twigs can be considered to be miniature trees in their own right. Such a hierarchy permits a tree to be described as a procedure, which builds a large structure from self-similar elements, and is described by procedural fractal geometry. Although this technique has been around for some time, Blueberry3D is the first commercial product to use procedural fractal geometry in real time.

Blueberry3D software was developed by Sjöland & Thyselius VR Systems in Sweden who have recently changed their name to Blueberry3D, and permits 3D terrain to be decorated with thousands of trees, bushes, shrubbery, and grass. Plates 19–22 show different examples. Normally, these objects are represented by half a dozen textured polygons, whereas Blueberry3D trees have trunks, branches, twigs, and leaves that move in the wind in real time! What is more, the closer you get to these fractal trees the more detail is revealed.

The system consists of two components:

- Blueberry3D Terrain Editor, which is a plug-in module to Creator Terrain Studio;
- the Blueberry3D Development Environment, which uses the Vega Scene Graph (VSG) of Vega Prime.

A full LynX Prime user interface and C++ API makes it easy to add Blueberry3D to any Vega Prime application. Compatibility against other third-party products such as DI-Guy from Boston Dynamics ensures access to a wide range of optional features (Plates 23 and 24).

6.5.1 Blueberry3D Terrain Editor

The Blueberry3D Terrain Editor allows the creation of material classified terrain using advanced fractal mathematics, and procedural geometry. The system allows the import of a wide range of geographical data formats and comes with an extensive feature database including trees, shrubbery, and surface materials.

6.5.2 Material Classification

A Blueberry3D database contains advanced material classified terrain where the system knows not only soil types but such features as erosion and density. The surface layers can consist of rock, soil, sand, shrubbery, trees, and so forth with their own special characteristics, and when they interact, objects like rocks will not be covered by soil or sand, and shrubs and trees will only grow on soil or sand.

6.5.3 Blueberry3D Development Environment

The Blueberry3D Development Environment is a fully integrated module to MultiGen-Paradigm's Vega Prime. Brief list of features:

- procedural geometry in real time;
- LynX Prime GUI interface;
- full C++ API;
- uses the VSG.

6.5.4 Collision Detection

Collision detection is a natural feature of Blueberry3D, which makes simulation and computer games natural applications. By adjusting Blueberry3D to conform to a motion model, higher performance and complexity can be achieved as the system takes into account the dynamics of the vehicle. A slow-moving tank compared to a helicopter can have very different optimization of the real-time database for greater performance at ground level. The motion model is also aware of what kind of terrain it is traversing as the database contains material information. This allows the vehicle to behave differently when driving over hard rock compared to soft sand.

6.5.5 Blueberry3D Summary

You may find the idea of moving through a 3D terrain in real time covered in rocks, trees, and shrubs with an LOD that enables you to see individual leaves that move in the wind difficult to believe. But take my word – it is possible. Just go to the Blueberry3d website and play some of their animations. You will not believe your eyes.

6.6 Boston Dynamics

Boston Dynamics was formed in 1992 as a spin-off from the Massachusetts Institute of Technology (MIT), where the company's founders had developed advanced robots and control systems. This experience provided the knowledge base for the dynamic human simulation software products now offered by Boston Dynamics, which include DI-Guy™, PeopleShop™, and DigitalBiomechanics™.

6.6.1 DI-Guy

DI-Guy is software for adding life-like human characters to real-time VEs. The user creates the characters and controls their behaviour using high-level function calls within a real-time environment such as OpenGL, Vega Prime or Performer. DI-Guy includes photo-realistic human models; an extensive library of over 1500 behaviours captured from real people; a real-time motion engine that uses the behaviour to make characters move realistically; and a simple API. Typical applications include:

- ground warfare, urban combat;
- counter-terrorist operations;
- law-enforcement training;
- flight deck operations;
- driver simulation and training;
- emergency response training;
- architectural visualization.

Figure 6.5 shows two views of an architectural scene populated by DI-Guy characters.

6.6.2 PeopleShop

PeopleShop is a tool for creating interactive 3D scenarios that feature groups of realistic people. The software enables the user to create, edit, and add new scenarios without programming. Typical applications include:

- catapult launch officer training;
- mission rehearsal training;
- emergency response trainer;
- law-enforcement training;

Figure 6.5 Two views of a VE populated by characters from the DI-Guy system. Image courtesy of Boston Dynamics.

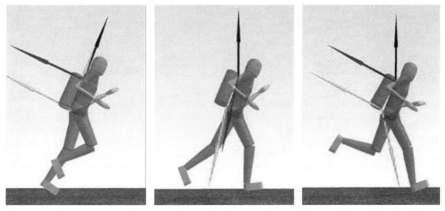

Figure 6.6 Three views created by the Digital Biomechanics system showing the magnitude and direction of forces generated by a running person. Image courtesy of Boston Dynamics.

- mission planning and training;
- nuclear power plant control room operator training.

6.6.3 DigitalBiomechanics

DigitalBiomechanics is a powerful software simulation tool that models the effect of equipment on soldiers engaged in real tasks, from walking, running, and crawling to completing a virtual obstacle course. It can be used to analyse the impact of prototype designs on soldier performance before building physical mockups and doing live testing.

The user can select model geometry from a US anthropometric database that includes over 4000 subjects, or by entering specific human measurements. This human geometry can be integrated with equipment geometry such as a back-pack fitted with straps, belts, and pads, and the combination evaluated for forces arising at moments of acceleration. The forces can be visualized as coloured vectors, which reveal their magnitude and direction. A typical scene is shown in Fig. 6.6.

6.7 MultiGen

Although I have said that many VR models are imported from CAD systems, there are a number of modelling systems that are used to create 3D VEs. Perhaps one of the most well-known companies in this field is MultiGen, Inc., who have been producing modelling software since 1986. Their products are widely used throughout the simulation, real-time, and entertainment industries, and their OpenFlight scene description database runs on SGI, E&S, CAE, Flight Safety, Sony, Nintendo, Sega, Macintosh, PCs and many other real-time 3D platforms. The software products include MultiGen II Pro, MultiGen Creator, MultiGen GO, and SmartScene.

6.7.1 MultiGen II Pro

MultiGen II Pro is a powerful interactive modelling system with many features that include:

- extruding and surfaces of revolution;
- auto-created LOD;
- geometry control at group, object, polygon and vertex level;
- polygon sorting for fast rendering;
- modelling of interactive instruments and control devices;
- attach sounds to 3D geometry;
- populate any selected area of the database with objects;
- data reduction;
- real-time preview;
- fog, lights, and weather effects.

6.7.2 MultiGen Creator

MultiGen's Creator system is founded on the OpenFlight scene description database format, and has been designed to meet the specific needs of the 3D, real-time, visualization, and simulation developer. Application areas include computer game development, architectural visualization, training simulators, and military simulation. Some of features include:

- modelling low polygon objects;
- collision detection;
- interactive texture mapping;
- free-form deformation of objects;
- associate sounds to 3D geometry;
- LOD creation and preview;
- spatial culling to fast rendering.

6.7.3 MultiGen SmartScene

MultiGen SmartScene users immersive VR to build a 3D database. The user wears a two-handed Fakespace Pinch Glove interface, and HMD, and interactively manipulates objects, textures, colours, and lights using hand gestures. The tasks of positioning, scaling, and rotating objects are done simultaneously in a single-hand gesture. Pinch Gloves use fingertip touch pads that provide the functionality of two four-button mice.

6.7.4 MultiGen Summary

As I have mentioned earlier, it is pointless for a VR system manufacturer to duplicate the 3D modelling tools currently available. Companies such as MultiGen have almost three decade's experience in designing and perfecting such software tools, and it is futile attempting to compete with them. MultiGen's software products have had an enormous impact on the simulation industry, and their OpenFlight standard is a ubiquitous format for representing 3D databases.

6.8 Summary

In this chapter I have attempted to show that software is the key to any successful VR system. Such software is very complex as it integrates the areas of 3D geometric databases, rendering, interaction, navigation, 3D tracking, graphics peripherals, sound, human factors, and interface design, all running in real time. But users of VR systems want much more than this. They want to use a VR system within their own area of specialism, which could be anything from a computer game to inspecting a CAD database of an offshore oil platform! This has meant that VR companies have had to develop generic software tools that can be applied to a wide variety of disciplines, which is no mean task.

In the next chapter we will explore various VR applications, and discover how the software requirement of one application is totally different to another.

7
VR Applications

7.1 Introduction

In the 1970s when computers first started to make some sort of impact, it was possible to see that their application would have long-term ramifications on all sorts of sectors. And although it was difficult to predict exactly what would happen, one knew that the world would never be the same again. Information systems, mathematical computation, graphic design, engineering design, aerospace, architecture, control systems, telecommunications, accounting, stock markets, and even fine art were all destined to be innocent victims for computerization.

In spite of some mistakes, it was an exciting period of discovery where the so-called 'computer experts' learned about their craft with every system they implemented. Software tools were very primitive and system design methodologies were invented *ad hoc*.

Almost 40 years later we can look back on this period with some satisfaction, for today the computer has become the most influential technological invention in human endeavour. Computers are everywhere, and we use them in all aspects of our daily lives. Today, we do not have to argue the case for using computers – it is a forgone conclusion that a computer solution is probably the best solution.

Now that our lives revolve around computers we are in the midst of a mini revolution: virtual reality (VR). VR, like computers, could touch everything to do with our daily lives, but it will not happen overnight. Like the early computer systems, VR will require time to mature before it can be applied effectively. Software, standards, and interfaces are all issues that must be addressed if VR is to become a ubiquitous technology. But we cannot just sit back and wait for these issues to be resolved – we must discover everything about VR in order to understand its strengths and weaknesses in order to influence its future.

Fortunately for everyone, some very dedicated people have realized that the only way to progress VR is to become involved and push the subject forward. But apart from pushing from within, VR needs to be pulled by the sectors that will eventually benefit from its use. It cannot be left to such a small industry to understand how every industrial sector can use their technology and develop appropriate software tools – it must be a joint effort.

To a certain extent this is now happening and various industries are exploring how best to use VR within their own sector. However, we must interpret carefully how such projects are progressing: great strides are being made, but VR is still an emerging technology, and we must learn to accept that it cannot be rushed.

With these thoughts in mind let us explore potential application areas for VR. The list will not be exhaustive but it will provide the opportunity to discuss a whole range of issues associated with VR and the way it is applied. Some of the examples are based on real case studies, while others are anticipating future scenarios.

7.2 Industrial

Today, computer-aided design (CAD) is an important tool for industry, and the idea of using a virtual representation of a three dimensional (3D) object is nothing new. Computers are used on a daily basis to design everything from a single gear to an entire aircraft. Some CAD workstations can manipulate 3D objects in real time, but as these databases become very large, real-time manipulation becomes difficult.

An engineer does not have to be persuaded of the importance of 3D visualization. Anything that minimizes the introduction of errors has to be considered, for the last thing anyone wants to commission is the production of an expensive tool, moulding or pressing, only to discover a design fault.

One of the major advantages of CAD is the ability to visualize an object before it is manufactured, but VR enables us to get one step closer by inspecting it in real time with the aid of a suitable display. However, this facility cannot be arbitrarily interfaced to the CAD process – it must be an integral feature. This will take time, but it is highly likely that VR visualization and inspection will become a standard feature of future CAD systems. Typical industrial applications for VR include:

- visualizing engineering concepts;
- training personnel;
- evaluating ergonomic issues;
- visualizing virtual prototypes;
- exploring servicing strategies;
- simulating the interaction of assemblies;
- simulating the dynamics of articulated structures;
- stress analysis;
- distributed product development management;

- simulating manufacturing processes;
- collaborative engineering on large AEC projects;
- machining and pressing simulation;
- concurrent engineering.

It is impossible to explore all of the above to the depth they deserve, but let us examine the idea of servicing, ergonomic, virtual prototypes, and visualizing engineering concepts.

7.2.1 Servicing Using a Virtual Prototype

Prior to CAD, engineering design involved designing and building a prototype before commissioning the tools to manufacture the real thing. The physical prototype was quite useful as it gave people something to relate to when considering its size, weight, centre of gravity, mechanical handling, manufacturing, and servicing issues. In many cases CAD made the physical prototype redundant, and substituted a virtual prototype in its place. With ever-increasing confidence in CAD, engineers are now able to bypass this design stage and hopefully save time and money. However, some structures being designed using CAD are very complex, and require careful examination before proceeding to the production stage. In some instances, such as the aero-engine industry, a physical prototype is constructed to verify the CAD model. With engines costing millions of dollars each, manufacturing, servicing, and operational issues have to be taken very seriously.

It is ironic though, that having used a computer to construct a complete virtual engine, a physical model has to be built to confirm the design! Alas this is so, but hopefully VR will provide a solution to avoid this expensive process. For instance, if the engine's database could be input into a VR system it would be possible to interact with various components and explore issues of manufacture and servicing. Although the principle is sound, it is not quite as easy as this. To begin with, the database is extremely large and is not in a format readily accepted by a VR system. But filters are available to make this conversion. The size of the database is a serious problem and currently the only way to process it is in partitions. Nevertheless, sufficient research has been undertaken to show that it is possible to perform specific tasks at a virtual level that confirm it is possible to assemble and service the engine.

One approach is to view the virtual engine using a head-mounted display (HMD) and interactive glove. Then with the aid of collision detection, attempt to retrieve various pipes and components without colliding with any other components. But anyone who has serviced a car will know only too well, that the major problem of undoing the simplest nut is access for one's arm and hand, and getting sufficient torque to the spanner. If VR is to be of any use to the aero-engine industry it must be able to simulate such manoeuvres accurately.

Division Ltd. provided an original solution to this problem by introducing a virtual mannequin into their dVISE software (Table 7.1). The immersed user stands alongside their 'Manikin Fred' and trains it to undertake a certain task. While Fred manipulates

Table 7.1 Universal Virtual Product using dVISE: Characteristics of Division's dVISE system.

Real-time performance	Real-time fly-through of large databases
3D interaction	Ability to pick and move objects
Collision detection	Real-time detection of colliding parts
CAD link	Run-time link to Pro-Engineer or Unigraphics
Moving parts	Create very complex assemblies/disassembles
Animation	Create and study assembly/disassembly sequences
Behaviour	Create complex physical simulations
Collaboration	Support multi-user (collaborative) sessions
Assemblies	View and edit entire assembly trees
Joints and linkages	Create joints between parts
Image fidelity	Create realistic images with materials and textures
Audio	Define realistic audio properties
Part information	Create part data lists
Selective importing	Only load those parts of an assembly you need
3D support	Supports 3D projection, CrystalEyes and Spaceball
Immersion	Support optional full immersion

Figure 7.1 Rolls Royce Trent 800 engine. Image courtesy of Virtual Presence.

a component with its arm and hand, the system looks for any interference with the database. When Fred is able to retrieve the component without collisions, it can be instructed to repeat the manoeuvre while the operator observes it from different points of view. Figure 7.1 shows a view of the Rolls Royce Trent 800 engine, which has been used to evaluate the use of VR techniques in its servicing requirements. The idea of the mannequin is a very powerful interactive paradigm and is explored further in the next example.

Figure 7.2   Manikin Fred being used to evaluate an F1 car. Image courtesy of Division Ltd.

7.2.2 Ergonomics

If we are to abandon physical mockups, whether they are aero-engines or bulldozers, then some ergonomic issues will have to be conducted at a virtual level. This does not mean that we will be able to sit on a virtual chair and discover if it is comfortable or not; or sit inside a virtual car and feel a virtual leather steering wheel! However, it does mean that we can place a virtual person on a virtual chair and discover whether their feet touch the ground; whether their back is strained; and whether there is support for their head. It also means that we can place our virtual driver inside a virtual car and discover if they can reach the steering wheel, and whether they have a safe view of the road. These seem impossible tasks but they are all possible, and much more!

For example, Fig. 7.2 shows how a manikin can be used to evaluate an F1 car. The manikin can be seated in the car and used to explore optimum positions for foot pedals, steering wheel, and instrumentation. It is also a simple exercise to see what it sees from his position.

7.2.3 Transom Jack

Transom Jack (TJ) is another solution to ergonomic problems and comes in the form of a biomechanically accurate human figure that works inside a virtual environment (VE).

Figure 7.3 TJ. Image courtesy of Transom Corporation.

TJ was born in the Center for Human Modeling and Simulation at the University of Pennsylvania, and is marketed by Transom Corporation.

TJ is used to resolve issues of fit and comfort, visibility, ingress and egress, reaching and grasping, foot pedal operation, multi-person interaction, user maintenance, and strength assessment. And when TJ is undertaking any of these tasks it is possible to look through the eyes and see exactly what is seen. When TJ walks, he moves with accurate body behaviour and balance control. And when TJ grasps an object, he uses fully articulated hands and 15 automatic grasps that adapt finger position to the object. TJ has the following characteristics:

- TJ has 74 segments, 73 joints, a realistic 22-segment spine, and 150 degrees of freedom (DOF);

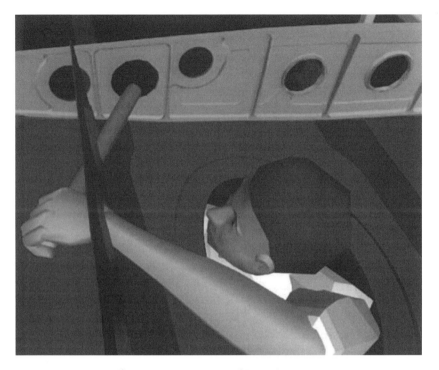

Figure 7.4 TJ. Image courtesy of Transom Corporation.

- TJ is derived from anthropometric data validated by the ANSUR 88 survey;
- the dimensions of TJ are based on 132 anthropometric measurements;
- TJ can be customized based on scaling;
- TJ obeys joint and strength limits taken from National Aeronautics and Space Administration (NASA) studies;
- TJ can be represented as a stick figure, wire frame, shaded, transparent, or solid.

Figure 7.3 shows TJ evaluating ergonomic issues when servicing an aircraft, and Fig. 7.4 shows TJ being used to evaluate access to components.

7.2.4 Virtual Prototypes

No one would dispute the importance of the virtual domain created by CAD systems. But this domain is now been extended by VR in all sorts of directions – in particular, the way it adds value at all stages in the product life cycle are as follows:

- provides rapid prototyping of early concepts;
- provides a presentation medium for managers and customers;
- reduces the need for detailed physical prototypes;
- improves product ergonomics and functionality;

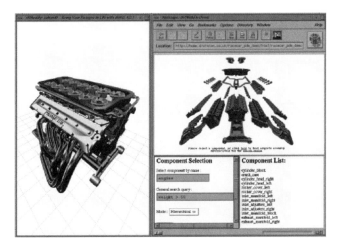

Figure 7.5   Using the Netscape browser to visualize a CAD database. Image courtesy of Division Ltd.

- supports concurrent engineering;
- provides manufacturing with early access to product details;
- creates cost-effective interactive training manuals;
- provides a cost-effective way to present product configuration and aesthetics.

The universality introduced by this design methodology supports collaborative design, and provides everyone with an increased understanding of complex 3D assemblies.

Today, designers no longer work in the same building: they may be on another site 30 miles away, or even in another country 3000 miles away. They may even work for another company sub-contracted to perform designated tasks. Managing such a distributed network requires new ideas, new tools, and new working modalities. But central to everything is computer software. Figure 7.5 illustrates an Internet browser being used to view a CAD database.

7.2.5 Virtual Weapons

GDE Systems and the US Army Armament Research Development and Engineering Center (ARDEC) used VR to optimize the design of virtual weapons. Such weapons are based on 3D solid models imported from Pro-Engineer CAD/CAM software. The models are integrated into a VE using Division's dVISE VR software running on an SGI Onyx workstation, and an HMD.

Several weapons have been evaluated with VR at ARDEC, including the Objective Individual Combat Weapon (OICW) and the M198 towed howitzer. The OICW is a multi-purpose, hand-held weapon and the VR simulation allows a user to interact with an urban scenario using a stereo-lithography model of the OICW.

The M198 howitzer (Fig. 7.6) simulation allows users to examine concept autoloader operations under battlefield-type conditions. As a result, ARDEC is capable of

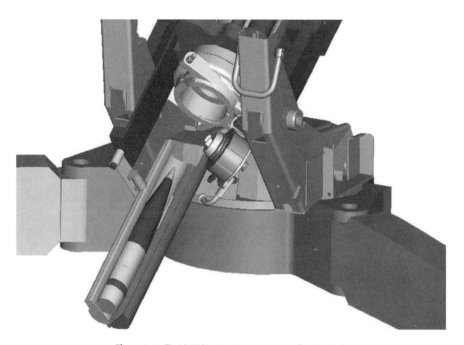

Figure 7.6   The M198 howitzer. Image courtesy of Division Ltd.

evaluating the feasibility of various autoloader designs. The OICW and M198 VR simulations, along with others under development, will ultimately become an integral part of distributed interactive simulation (DIS) node of ARDEC. This will allow users to be immersed in a simulated battlefield using hardware that is still in the concept development stage.

7.2.6 Visual Engineering

Eveva Ltd (formerly the Cadcentre Ltd.) at Cambridge, UK, has pioneered the use of CAD since its inception. Today, they have embraced the technology of VR and are pioneering the use of group VR in process plant design using their RealityWave software, and the use of a panoramic screen.

The Eveva's Plant Design Management System (PDMS) is used throughout the world in the design of offshore platforms, chemical processing plant, oil refineries, nuclear facilities, etc. But a PDMS database can now be used by RealityWave to visualize massive 3D structures in real time. The advantages are enormous, as it makes it easier for project staff and other personnel to assess, and become familiar with design proposals, planned operational changes, maintenance tasks, and escape routes.

7.2.7 Spatial Visualization

Visualizing spatial problems is what VR is about. Whether it is trying to understand the 3D electrical bonds of a complex molecule or navigating the interior of a proposed

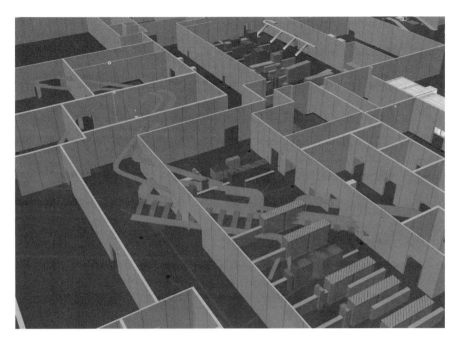

Figure 7.7   A simulated production plant layout for Northern Foods. Image courtesy of PERA.

offshore oil platform. VR provides intuitive ways for exploring 3D environments, no matter what they may be.

One such visualization problem that faces any industry is factory reorganization. It is a complex process as it involves optimizing parameters such as overall efficiency, machine accessibility, health and safety, services, etc. But it is the 3D nature of the problem that makes finding an optimum solution so difficult. Now VR is no magic wand, but it does provide a means for solving such problems effectively.

Such techniques were used by PERA to solve 3D spatial problems. One project involved redeveloping the internal production facility for Northern Foods. They wanted a further automated line in place of an existing manually intensive one, and the opportunity to reorganize the production flow.

PERA provided a detailed visualization of the entire production process, a means of delivering offline training and familiarization, and a visual production process simulation. The simulation was able to review the space utilization and production layout to assist the installation of the new production equipment and rearrangement of the existing plant. Site facilities such as drains, water supplies, and structural limitations were simulated and taken into account when positioning the new lines. All of this was done at a virtual level, in real time, avoiding any disruptions in factory production. Figure 7.7 shows an image from the real-time simulation of the factory production facility.

A similar problem was resolved by PERA when they were commissioned to simulate the new headquarters for Barclaycard. Barclaycard wanted their staff to see what their

Figure 7.8   A scene from a real-time simulation for Barclaycard's new Head Quarters. Image courtesy of PERA.

working environment would be like before they started construction. PERA took the CAD database of the architectural model and input it into their VR system. Some of the 2500 Barclaycard staff had the opportunity to view the virtual building and input ideas on the design of the offices, including floor layout, colour schemes, furnishing, and accessibility. Figure 7.8 shows a scene from the simulation.

7.3 Training Simulators

Simulators play a vital role in training personnel in all sorts of sectors and include airplanes, trains, lorries, tanks, medicine, ships, air traffic control towers, nuclear power stations, military weapons, etc. They are very effective and are used in areas where the only alternative is the actual system, which would be far too dangerous. The two applications selected for further description are medicine and aviation.

7.3.1 Medicine

Computers have had an incredible impact on medicine and health care, ranging from automatic systems to monitor patients to the image processing of 3D computerized tomography (CT) data. But one application that has captured the imagination of everyone is surgical training, and the role VR could play in simulating virtual organs, or an entire virtual cadaver.

7.3.1.1 *Soft Body Modelling*

There are some very difficult problems to overcome before we see VR systems widely used throughout the medical profession. The first one concerns the modelling of flesh and simulating its behaviour. The 3D models we have discussed in previous chapters were rigid, and in some cases incorporated articulated features. It is possible to model non-rigid bodies using triangles, but instead of using triangles of a fixed size, their size is allowed to change depending on the forces applied their vertices.

For example, in Fig. 7.9 a mesh of 3D triangles are interconnected with an element that changes its distance depending on the applied forces. Internally, the element has elastic and resistive properties that can be adjusted to simulate a variety of elastic materials. This is a useful strategy for modelling cloth and boundary surfaces that have elastic properties. However, because the mesh forms a thin skin, its interior is empty and is not convenient to model a solid piece of flesh. Another approach is to model a 3D lattice of points that are interconnected with the same elements, as shown in Fig. 7.10.

When forces are applied to the lattice nodes, the 3D geometry adjusts to an appropriate new shape. And when the forces are removed, the geometry returns to its original shape, and could even oscillate slightly to simulate real-world behaviour. What is important is to adjust the parameters of the element to achieve a desired behaviour.

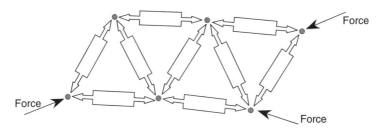

Figure 7.9   A flexible 3D triangular.

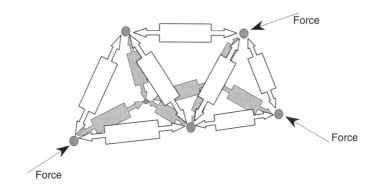

Figure 7.10   A flexible 3D lattice.

If the lattice structure is very fine it is even possible to arrange for a fault to propagate across the lattice to simulate a cutting action. Thus, a single lattice could be divided into two. So, basically, a strategy exists to model 3D flesh, and research is underway to perfect its implementation. In the meantime, though VR is still able to play a role in surgical training, we will take a brief look at a VR-based laparoscopic simulator.

7.3.1.2 *Minimally Invasive Surgery*

Minimally invasive surgery, or keyhole surgery using its popular name, is a surgical procedure that minimizes patient trauma by keeping body incisions as small as possible. In many cases, the incision is no more than 1 or 2 cm in diameter – just enough room to insert a surgical instrument. As the incision is so small the surgeon is unable to see what is taking place within the body's cavity, therefore another incision is made through which is passed an endoscope. The video output of the endoscope is displayed on a monitor and provides the surgeon with an internal view of the patient and the end of the keyhole instrument.

Naturally, this requires the surgeon to undertake surgical manoeuvres by looking at a screen rather than their hands, and calls for a different level of eye–hand spatial coordination. Furthermore, the endoscope provides a magnified view of the patient's interior and a narrow field of view (FOV).

In order to acquire the extra skills for keyhole surgery, surgeons use various physical training devices. These consist of simple trainers where a surgeon has to perform various tasks such as suturing, peeling grapes, manipulating small objects, etc. using laparoscopic tools. More sophisticated simulators use animal meat, and in some countries, live animals have been used.

In the early 1990s various VR-based laparoscopic simulators emerged but failed to convince the medical sector that a solution had been found. Today, things have improved and there is a deeper understanding of what the medical profession requires. It is still impossible to simulate gall bladders, hearts, kidneys, and other organs with the fidelity of their physical counterparts, and that will not happen for some years to come. However, we have reached a point where simple VR simulators can play a valuable role in the overall training task.

One such device is minimally invasive surgical training (MIST) from Virtual Presence Ltd. The system (Fig. 7.11) comprises of a frame holding two standard laparoscopic instruments, which are electronically linked, to a high-performance computer. MIST software constructs a VE on the screen showing the position and movement of the surgical instruments in real time.

In training mode, the program guides the trainee through a series of six tasks that become progressively more complex, enabling him or her to develop psychomotor skills essential for safe clinical practice. Each task is based on a key surgical technique employed in minimally invasive surgery. An online help facility, which includes video clips of live procedures, enables the trainee to relate the virtual task to its clinical context. The help facility also enables the trainee to use the system independently of the tutor.

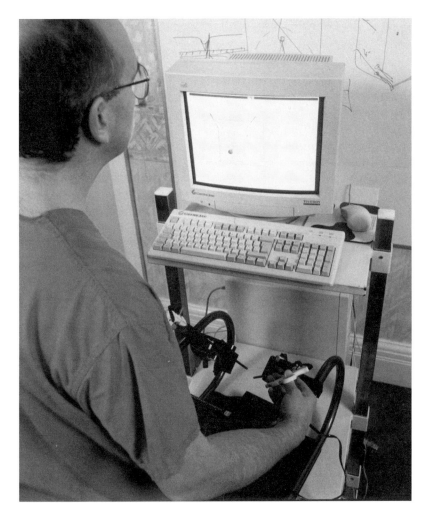

Figure 7.11   The MIST trainer in action. Image courtesy of Virtual Presence.

Performance is scored for time, errors, and efficiency of movement for each task, and for both right and left hands. This information is available on completion of the tasks for the trainee, and is stored to the database for review by the tutor. The ultimate goal for laparoscopic simulators is to provide realistic force feedback from the surgical instruments, realistic 3D VEs, running in real time on a low-cost platform.

A similar type of simulator has been developed at the University of Hull, UK, but simulates surgical operations on the knee. Figure 7.12 shows the simulator in action. It consists of an artificial knee with appropriate keyhole instruments. On the table, the trainee surgeon observes the interior of a virtual knee, complete with virtual instruments. As the real instruments are manipulated, tracking devices hidden within the false knee relay their position to a host computer that responds in real time with an updated view of the virtual knee.

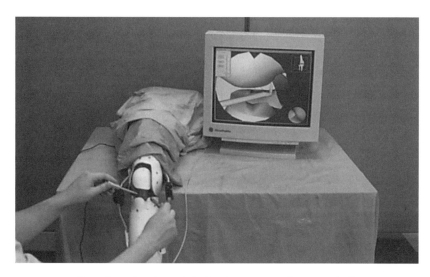

Figure 7.12   An arthroscopic simulator. Image courtesy of University of Hull.

INRIA in France is also developing a surgical simulator for liver hepatectomy in close collaboration with the IRCAD Centre. Geometric models of the liver and of the portal vein are obtained through the automatic segmentation of real patient 3D CT scan images. The parenchyma is represented as a tetrahedral mesh and its physical behaviour is simulated using a finite element method. This enables the system to support real-time tissue deformation, volumetric cutting, vessel management, and force feedback.

It is not difficult to appreciate the importance of these systems, and as computers become cheaper and new software systems developed, VR simulators will become a natural part of any surgeon's training.

7.3.1.3 *Virtual Therapy*

For those suffering from acrophobia (fear of heights) the Kaiser-Permanente Medical Group in Marin County, California offers an interesting treatment using VR. Dr Ralph Lamson at the medical group used 90 volunteers in an experimental study, of whom, 90% reached their self-assigned 'height goals'.

The volunteers were placed in a VE where they encountered the perception of depth and height. The environment depicted a café with an elevated patio and plank leading from the patio to a bridge. Surrounding hills and water completed the scene. Forty-four of the participants in the study were selected randomly to immerse themselves in this environment using Division's Pro Vision 100 VR system.

Under the guidance of Lamson, each volunteer was given an HMD that depicted the VE. The challenge was to exit the café onto the patio, move across the plank, and explore the bridge. As they approached the edge of the plank and the bridge and looked at the landscape below, heart rate and blood pressure were measured to monitor the level of anxiety. After successfully 'surviving' their virtual encounter with heights and depths, the participants graduated to real-world goals, such as driving across a bridge and going inside a glass enclosed elevator while looking outside.

7.3.2 Civilian Flight Simulators

Throughout this book I have referred to the way the flight simulation industry paved the way for many VR techniques, so maybe it is time to elaborate slightly on this application.

A flight simulator has two important roles: one is to assess the technical competence of qualified pilots, and the other is to familiarize qualified pilots with a new craft. Flight simulators are expensive (typically $10m), and their running costs are equally high; consequently their usage has to be carefully organized.

Inside the simulator is a replica cockpit of a specific aircraft. The layout and dimensions of every instrument and panel are so accurate that it is easy to accept it as the real thing – even though it may only be constructed from wood! The instruments are connected to a computer that simulates the complete behaviour of the plane: from the heat characteristics of the engines to the pneumatic properties of the undercarriage. Thus when a pilot starts the virtual engines, the relevant instruments respond with their temperature and fuel consumption.

This computer is able to replicate the electrical and mechanical characteristics of the plane, but another computer is required to create the images seen through the cockpit window. Although it is a computer, it is dedicated to the task of image generation – hence its name, *Image Generator* (IG). A VE of an airport and the surrounding terrain are loaded into the IG, together with the position of the simulated plane. Then, as the pilot goes through a takeoff procedure, the IG is updated with the changing position of the plane and responds with appropriate images at 60 Hz update rate. As the plane gathers speed down the runway, another computer is waiting to simulate the flying characteristics of the craft using a mathematical model provided by the plane's manufacturer. As soon as the pilot manoeuvres the plane into a takeoff attitude, the virtual plane leaves the virtual runway and the mathematical flying model takes over.

Meanwhile, during the takeoff, the IG has been supplied with the real-time position of the virtual plane, and has responded with realistic images that surround the cockpit 150° horizontally and 50° vertically. The pilot is inside a cockpit that is indistinguishable from the real thing; there are real-time collimated images outside the cockpit windows; the cabin resonates to the surround sound of jet engines; and a 6-DOF motion platform moves the ten-ton platform to provide accurate motion cues. This is real immersion! Figure 2.12 shows a modern full-flight simulator.

But in such a mission, a pilot and co-pilot are being assessed to see if they can cope with the unexpected. And inside the cabin is a trainer – an experienced pilot, whose role is to perform the assessment process. His task is relatively easy, because inside the cabin, out of sight from the pilots, is a touch sensitive screen that connects to the IG and the host computers. Simply by touching part of the screen, the trainer can activate

Figure 7.13   Royal Brunei Airlines Boeing 767-300 Full-Flight Simulator. Image courtesy Thomson Training & Simulation.

a virtual engine fire, a faulty undercarriage, a leaking fuel pump, etc., and then waits to observe how the pilot and co-pilot respond. The touch screen can also be used to interact with the 3D VE: another plane can be moved onto the runway during a landing scenario; another plane can be flown along a collision course; and even a storm can be introduced and cover the runway with virtual snow! Figure 7.13 shows the cockpit interior of a Boeing 767-300 full-flight simulator used by the Royal Brunei Airlines.

The VEs will comprise an airport and the surrounding terrain, and can easily cover 50 square miles, which requires several levels of detail. For example, when the plane is making a final approach to the runway, the terrain below can consist of an aerial or satellite photograph of the area. In the distance, the pilot sees the airport and its illu-minated runway, which are modelled at low resolution to keep the polygon count to a minimum. As the airport becomes larger, extra detail is faded in to reveal new fea-tures of buildings. Finally, when the plane touches the runway, the motion platform responds with an appropriate movement, and forces are fed back through the flight controls. As the pilot drives towards a terminal building, the IG is checking to ensure that the virtual wings are not touching buildings or any other planes. When the plane finally comes to a halt in front of the docking station, one can even see virtual people inside the terminal pushing their luggage along corridors, just to complete the picture. Figure 7.14 shows a scene depicting a virtual airport as the simulated plane approaches its docking area.

The entire experience is overwhelming – and it has to be – for without this attention to detail, it would not be possible to create the necessary level of presence and immersion that make the flight simulator such an effective training tool.

Figure 7.14 Airport scene produced by an E&S IG. Image courtesy of Evans & Sutherland Computer Corporation, Salt Lake City, Utah, USA.

7.3.3 Military Flight Simulators

Military flight simulators rely upon similar technology, but tend to use a dome as the display surface, as this replicates the all-round vision they have in a modern fighter. More projectors and IGs are required to cover the extra surface of the dome, but they do not have to display high-resolution images. By tracking the pilot's eyes, it is possible to have a medium-resolution background image with a high-resolution gaze image. Thus, wherever the pilot looks, there will be appropriate detail.

In combat, pilots are flying extremely fast and must be familiar with the surrounding terrain, which means that the mission rehearsal simulator must also reflect this level of accuracy. To resolve this problem, satellite images are used, which provide height as well as texture information. When processed by software tools such as RapidScene/Freedom of E&S, it is possible to convert a numerical data file into a realistic terrain as seen in Fig. 7.15.

7.4 Entertainment

Real-time computer graphics plays a central role in computer games, arcade games, and theme park experiences. In all three markets the technology is carefully chosen to entertain and create profit. Computer games cost about $50 and can provide many hours of entertainment – even a computer game station is relatively cheap.

Figure 7.15   A 3D database derived from a satellite image. Image courtesy of Evans & Sutherland Computer Corporation, Salt Lake City, Utah, USA.

Arcade games cost many times more but have to be much more robust and offer a more thrilling experience, and succeed in enticing the punter to have 'just one more go' in an attempt to improve upon a previous record.

Some early attempts to introduce immersive VR entertainment systems into the marketplace failed because of irreconcilable commercial factors. For example, a computer graphics workstation was often used as the real-time source of images, which immediately made it impossible to recoup its cost, let alone any other important features. When cheaper graphics boards emerged and low-cost HMDs were designed, it still seemed impossible to maintain the necessary throughput to generate a valid commercial return. But as the VR industry progresses, new and hopefully commercially viable products are appearing.

7.4.1 Dream Glider and Sky Explorer

Dreamality Technologies, Inc. is a manufacturer of VR-based simulators for hang gliding, paragliding, ultralights and other aviation simulators. Their Dream Glider system (Plate 27) replicates the performance of an actual hang glider, and is used by new hang glider pilots to improve their flying skills.

Figure 7.16   A VR seat manufactured by Dreamality Technologies. Image courtesy of Dreamality Technologies.

The rider is free to fly anywhere within a VE, and a scoring system encourages the rider to fly to a landing area and land safely. The rider scores points for finding thermals and gaining altitude, the length of flying time, and for successful landings. The scoring system also deducts points for crashes and collisions with weather phenomena and objects such as planes, jets, birds, balloons, ultralights, buildings, etc.

The Dream Glider is personal computer (PC) based and allows the rider to experience the normal flying sensations of sound, tactile, motion cues, and visual feedback. When using a HMD, head tracking can be used to permit the rider to look in any direction, and when networked to other simulators, each rider can see fellow riders in their environment.

The ultralight Sky Explorer is a motion-based simulator with pitch and roll in the basic product. Plate 28 shows the motion system, which includes throttle and rudder pedals.

The Sky Explorer can also be networked with the Dream Glider so that users can see each other in their own visual display. They can interact with each other, fly coordinated manoeuvres, or even try to knock each other out of their virtual skies! The VEs currently available include: Space, Islands, Jungle, Volcano, Castles, Obstacles, Swamp, Frontier, Prehistoric, and City. Two such VEs are shown in Plates 25 and 26.

Another interesting system from Dreamality is their VR seat shown in Fig. 7.16. The seat is fitted to a small motion system driven by a PC, which enables it to be easily interfaced to VR software.

7.5 VR Centres

Silicon Graphics continue to pioneer VR centres which are equipped with state-of-the-art technology for interpreting 3D data sets. Using their high-performance computers and panoramic screens, clients can be 'flown' through their virtual projects

Figure 7.17   A scene from a real-time visualisation of an airport. Image courtesy of the VR Centre at Teesside University.

Figure 7.18   A scene from a real-time train driver simulator. Image courtesy of the VR Centre at Teesside University.

Figure 7.19   A virtual gymnast. Image courtesy of the VR Centre at Teesside University.

and inspect them at their leisure. Such a service is probably one that will develop into a sustainable commercial activity. For there will always be industrial sectors who do not wish to personally become involved with VR, but are prepared to purchase the services of experts who have access to the very latest technology.

The VR Centre at Teesside University was established to offer local industry with access to sophisticated VR systems and support services. The centre owns a variety of systems that include two hemispherical domes, screens, HMDs, a large motion capture facility, and a variety of VR software tools. Prospective clients simply have to submit their data to the centre and then attend sessions where they can undertake their visual assessment in real time. Clients can also take away an animated record of their VE so that it can be shared with third parties.

Typical projects include interior design (Plate 29), urban development (Plate 30), airport design (Fig. 7.17), a train driver simulator (Fig. 7.18), and human movement analysis (Fig. 7.19).

7.6 Summary

There has only been space to investigate some of the applications for VR that are currently underway. Unfortunately, some had to be left out, such as architecture, fashion, automotive design, education, training, science, space, etc., and if these were your areas of specialism I apologize. But hopefully, the applications I have covered will give you an insight and the potential of VR technology in other areas.

What I have tried to do in this chapter is to show that VR has matured very quickly and offers powerful solutions to some very difficult problems. VR is no longer a technology looking for an application; it is a solution to any problem that involves the real-time visualization of complex 3D data.

It is not difficult to imagine how car-body designers, architects, or fashion designers could use VR. The technology exists – it is just a question of developing appropriate software tools.

8
Conclusion

8.1 The Past

It is strange to look back and recall the manual techniques used to design everything from a bracket to a complete aircraft. A large wooden drawing board with T-square, pair of compasses, a set-square, a set of plastic French curves, an eraser, etc. were the typical tools of the draftsman. Specialist skills were required in projections, cross sections, developed surfaces, and perspective views. And to obtain a realistic view of the final artefact, a technical artist was used to render a coloured image.

Then computers came along, and the discipline of computer graphics was born. A new set of design tools emerged that relieved the draftsman from the tedious pencil-based tasks. Computer graphics showed that it was capable of undertaking all of the manual tasks associated with three-dimensional (3D) design, from which emerged the sophisticated computer-aided design (CAD) systems we use today. But computer graphics did not stop evolving. Computer graphics was used to animate two-dimensional (2D) shapes and 3D objects, and computer animation was born which blossomed into the industry of digital special effects. Another target was video and television, and the computer demonstrated amazing dexterity in its ability to manipulate real-time video. Video images could be painted, retouched, enhanced, cut and pasted, turned like a real page, until it was impossible to tell whether they were real or synthetic.

Having mastered images, computers were used to process sound, from which evolved multimedia systems to provide a unifying digital medium for text, sound, and images. But computers did not stop evolving. Faster, cheaper, and smaller systems kept appearing each year, making the computerization of new markets cost-effective solutions.

All of these developments were taking place against a backdrop of rapid technological advances in electronics, miniaturization, new materials, communications, etc., making possible totally new computer-based systems. One of these developments was virtual reality (VR) that offered a new way of interacting with the complex 3D structures being stored inside computers.

8.2 Today

Today, we take for granted CAD systems. We do not think twice about the fact that we are using digital packets of electricity and magnetism to encode and manipulate 3D objects. Designs of buildings, cars, robots, household objects, and even circuits for new computers, are designed with such efficiency and familiarity, that one could believe it was the only way to undertake such tasks.

However, even though these systems are so effective, we continue to refine and extend these tools with even more powerful tools, one of which is VR. But as we have seen, VR is not restricted to the world of CAD, that is, it has applications that know no boundaries. VR can be used in computer games, education, training, simulation, visualization, surgery, and a hundred-and-one other topics.

8.3 Conclusion

If you have managed to read through the previous seven chapters, you should have formed an opinion about what VR is and how it works. I have tried to present to you what I believe to be the essential elements of VR, free from any popular journalistic hype – just the facts. Now this might not have tallied with your original perception of VR, and my description may not have supported some of the fantastic stories that surround VR – but that was not my aim. Even at this stage of the book I could fantasize about the role of VR in the current millennium, but I do not know what purpose that would serve. Anyone can make predictions about the future, but when one is concerned with the present, then one must be accurate and honest.

I have shown that VR is a natural development in the progression of computer graphics. Yes, it introduces some strange concepts such as the ability to see, touch, and hear things that have no physical substance, but these experiences are obviously synthetic. VR was not developed to provide us with an alternative to the physical world, that is, it was developed to solve specific technical problems.

We have seen that the flight simulation industry has been major users of real-time graphics for many years. They have worked with the ideas of 3D models, dynamic level of detail, collision detection, force-feedback, immersive displays, interactive features, etc., long before the term *virtual reality* was coined. For them, they were dealing with simulation.

But over the last two decades it has become possible to implement many of these ideas on low-cost systems and apply them to a wider range of applications. But before any real serious work could be done, various books and films appeared that extrapolated VR in all sorts of directions. We were exposed to a world where we could navigate massive 3D corporate databases and cause havoc by destroying data using virtual weapons; one could wrestle with avatars; and why not be possessed by virtual intelligence! Authors and film directors created a fantastic world of VR that has become confused with the *real* world of VR.

I have mentioned in the opening chapter that the word 'virtual' has been totally over-used. And almost every day, articles appear in national newspapers concerning a new application for VR, creating an impression of a technology that is widely used in industry, commerce, medicine, training, military, and entertainment. This is far from the truth. Personally I would like this to be the case, because I am totally convinced by the benefits of VR. But one cannot force a technology upon any sector, whether it is VR or any other new invention.

When I prepared the original text for this last chapter, advertisements were appearing in the press announcing a new range of 500-MHz PC processors. Today, as I prepare this second edition, twin 3-GHz processors are the norm. There is no doubt that they outperform computers sold last year, but there is no way that any industry can afford to replace their existing computers with every new model that appears. The same thing is true with VR. No matter how compelling the reasons might be for using VR, it will take time to introduce VR into all of the relevant sectors of application. It will happen, and it will be a success, but it will happen in its own time.

Glossary

3D pointer   The visual representation of the user's hand as distinct from the ordinary mouse or text cursor; also known as the body.

Accommodation   The ability of the eye to alter the shape of its lens to focus on objects near and far.

Active environment   A virtual environment (VE) that includes events that are independent of the user.

Acuity   The ability to resolve fine detail.

Active matrix LCD   A liquid crystal display (LCD) with pixels controlled by discrete transistors.

Additive colour mixing   Creating colours by mixing two or three different coloured lights.

Additive primary colours   Red, green, and blue.

Aliasing

   (*a*) *Spatial*: Visual artefacts (such as jagged edges) caused by insufficient sampling.

   (*b*) *Temporal*: Animation artefacts (such as 'wagon wheels' apparently rotating backwards) caused by insufficient temporal sampling.

Ambient light   The background-level illumination introduced to illuminate a VE.

Ambisonics   A technique for recording sound using a Soundfield microphone, and played back using several loudspeakers.

Anechoic   Without echoes.

Angle of view   The solid angle of incident light transmitted by a lens.

Angular velocity   The rotational velocity about an axis.

Anti-aliasing   Strategies for removing or reducing aliasing artefacts arising from insufficient spatial or temporal sampling.

Anti-clockwise polygon   A polygon which has its interior to the left when its boundary is traversed in the direction of its edges.

Aspect ratio   Ratio of the vertical to the horizontal dimensions of an image or shape.

Attributes   Object properties, such as colour, surface texture, and mass.

Augmented reality   Display systems that mix synthetic images with views of the real world.

Authoring tool   See **Generator**.

Avatar   The abstract representation of the user in a VE.

Back face   The unseen side of a polygon.

Back-face removal   The removal of all back-facing polygons before a scene is rendered.

Back-projection screen   A translucent screen where the image is projected from behind.

Binaural   The use of two separate audio channels.

Binocular depth cues   Strategies such as eye convergence and parallax for estimating the distance of an object.

Binocular disparity   The differences between the left and right views of a scene.

Binocular vision   The ability to see two independent views of a scene.

Boom display   A display system mounted on a balanced articulated arm.

Boundary representation   A modelling strategy where objects are represented by a boundary skin.

Bounding box   A rectangular bounding volume that completely contains an object.

Bounding sphere   A spherical bounding volume that contains an object.

Browser   A computer program that interprets virtual reality modelling language (VRML) files and allows the user to interact and navigate them.

B-spline space curve   A smooth parametric curve whose shape is determined by a string of control points.

B-spline surface patch   A smooth parametric surface patch whose shape is determined by a matrix of control points.

Bump map   A two-dimensional (2D) image for making a surface appear bumpy.

C   A computer programming language.

C++   An object-oriented version of C.

CAD   An acronym for computer-aided design.

CAM   An acronym for computer-aided manufacture.

Cartesian coordinates   Two- or three-dimensional (2D or 3D) offset measurement relative to some defined origin and system of orthogonal axes.

Centre of projection   The point through which all projection lines pass.

CFD   See **Computational fluid dynamics**.

CFF   See **Critical fusion frequency**.

Ciliary muscles   Adjust the shape of the human eye's lens.

Clipping   Removes unwanted objects from a scene.

Clockwise polygon   A polygon which has its interior to the right when its boundary is traversed in the direction of its edges.

Cochlea   Converts sound pressure waves into nerve signals in the inner ear.

Collimated   A collimated optical system has light rays that appear to come from some distance.

Collision avoidance   Strategies to prevent objects from colliding.

Collision detection   Strategies to detect collisions between virtual objects.

Colour attributes   Colour values assigned to an object to enable it to be rendered.

Colour bleeding   When the colour of one object is reflected in another.

Colour model   A colour space such as red, green, and blue (RGB) or hue, saturation, and value (HSV).

Computational fluid dynamics (CFD)   Simulates the dynamic flow of gas and fluid about an object.

Cone   A receptor in the retina responsible for colour vision.

Constraints   Physical limits used to restrict behaviour of an object.

Constructive solid geometry (CSG)   A modelling strategy for building objects using the Boolean operators: union, subtraction and difference.

Cornea   The transparent surface at the front of the eye.

CPU   An acronym for central processing unit.

Critical fusion frequency   The frequency at which a flashing image appears continuous to the eye.

CRT   An acronym for cathode ray tube used for television and computer screens.

CSG   See **Constructive solid geometry**.

Culling   The action of identifying and removing objects from a view of a scene.

Cyberspace   A popular name given to the virtual 3D domain.

Database   A collection of related records organized such that particular classes of records are easily accessed.

Deep sensations   Measure pressure and pain, using receptors deep within body tissue.

Depth buffer   See **Z-buffer**.

Depth cues   Strategies used by the brain to estimate depth.

Depth of field   The distance over which an in-focus image is created in a lens.

Digitizer   A system for capturing 2D or 3D Cartesian coordinates.

dVISE   Division's virtual world simulation and authoring software tool.

dVS   Division's VR runtime environment.

Dynamic constraints   Physical constraints associated with moving objects such as mass and inertia.

Dynamic vertices   Vertices that can change their position in a VE.

Eardrum   A thin membrane in the middle ear that moves in sympathy with incoming sound pressure waves.

Edge   A line formed where two polygons meet.

Elastic collisions   Are associated with colliding rigid objects.

Environment mapping   A rendering technique where background reflections are seen in an object's surface.

Ergonomics   Using human dimensions in a design process.

Exoskeleton   An articulated structure surrounding part of our body to measure joint angles.

External sound stage   Externalizing sound sources outside our head.

Exteroceptive sensations   Touch sensations detected over our body surface.

Extruding   A modelling technique where a 2D cross section is used to create a 3D volume.

Eye convergence   The ability to rotate our eyes and focus upon an object.

Eye divergence   The action of moving both eyes outwards.
Eye relief   The distance between the user's face and the optics of an HMD.
Eye tracking   The technique of monitoring the gaze direction of the eye.

FEA   See **Finite element analysis**.
FFD   See **Free-form deformation**.
Field   The odd or even lines of a video frame.
Field of view (FOV)   The largest solid angle where incident light can form an image.
File   A collection of related data.
Finite element analysis (FEA)   A technique for simulating dynamic stresses in an object.
Fixating   The deliberate action of gazing at a point in space.
Flat screen view   A VE displayed in a window on a computer screen.
Flat shading   A process where a polygon is shaded with a single colour.
Flicker   Occurs when an image is not refreshed fast enough.
Flight simulator   A VE for training and evaluating pilots.
Flying   The action of moving from part of the VE to another.
Force feedback   Applying forces to the user's fingers, arm, or shoulder.
FOV   See **Field of view**.
Fovea   The high-resolution central zone in the retina.
Frame   Two fields of a video image, or a single rendering of a 3D world.
Frame store   A memory device for storing one video frame.
Free-form deformation (FFD)   A technique for distorting 2D and 3D objects.
Front face   The side of a polygon containing the surface normal.
Fusion frequency   The frequency when a flashing image appears continuous to the human visual system.

Gaze direction   The viewer's eye direction.
Generator   A computer program that creates VRML files. Synonymous with authoring tools.
Geometry   A description of the shape of an object and its surface characteristics.
Gesture recognition   The recognition of hand gestures made by the VR user.
Gouraud shading   A shading technique that interpolates colour over a surface.
Graphical user interface (GUI)   A graphics-based user interface.
Graph plotter   A device for creating line-based drawings.
Graphic primitive   A shape or object used by a graphic system to construct more complex scenes.
GUI   See **Graphical user interface**.

Hand tracking   The action of monitoring the position and orientation of the human hand.
Haptic   Synonomous with touch and force.
Head-mounted display (HMD)   A display system attached to the user's head.
Head-related transfer functions (HRTFs)   Encode the physical influence the upper torso have on incoming sound pressure waves.

Head tracking The action of monitoring the position and orientation of a human head.

Heave The vertical translation of a motion platform.

Hidden-surface removal A rendering strategy for removing invisible or masked surfaces.

HMD See **Head-mounted display**.

HRTF See **Head-related transfer functions**.

HSV Hue, saturation, and value colour model.

HTML Hyper-text markup language. A file specification supporting hyperlinks.

Hue The attribute given to a colour that describes its relative position within the visible spectrum.

Human factors The issues pertaining to human behaviour such as sight, sound, touch, and equilibrium.

Hyperlink A reference to a URL that is associated with an anchor node.

Hz Means cycles/second. Named after the scientist Hertz.

IG See **Image generator**.

Iggo dome receptor Touch receptors with a slow rate of adaptation.

Illumination model Describes how light is emitted, reflected, transmitted, and absorbed within a virtual world.

Image generator (IG) A computer capable of rendering real-time images.

Image plane Synonymous with the picture plane.

Immersion The sensation of being part of a VE.

Immersive VR A VR system where the user is immersed with a VE through the use of an immersive display.

Instance A reference to a master object.

Interactive computer graphics A computer interface that supports real-time, two-way, graphical interaction.

Interactive glove A glove that monitors finger and hand gestures.

Internal sound stage The internalization of a sound source.

Internet The worldwide named network of computers that communicates with each other using a common set of communication protocols known as TCP/IP.

Inter-ocular distance The distance between the optical centres of our eyes.

Interpenetrating objects When one virtual object intersects another.

Intranet A private network that uses the same protocols and standards as the Internet.

Inverse kinematics Modelling the movement of a jointed limb, such as an arm or leg.

I/O An acronym for input/output.

Iris The pigmented, opaque circular structure positioned in front of the eye's lens.

Joystick A device for monitoring hand movements.

JPEG Joint Photographic Experts Group.

Lag See **Latency**.

Laparoscopic simulator A training simulator for 'key-hole' surgery.

Laparoscopy Surgery undertaken through small incisions in the side of the body.

Latency The time delay (or lag) between activating a process and its termination.

LCD See **Liquid crystal display**.

LED See **Light emitting diode**.

Level of detail (LOD) The amount of detail or complexity displayed in a scene.

Light adaptation When the eye adjusts to a bright environment, having been adapted to low light levels.

Light emitting diode (LED) A semiconductor device that emits light on the application of a voltage.

Light source A virtual source of illumination used by the renderer to calculate light levels on a surface.

Liquid crystal display (LCD) Employs liquid crystals whose molecules can be oriented to different positions by the application of an electric field.

Macula Hair cells in the utricle within the vestibular system for sensing gravity.

Material A definition of the surface characteristics of an object, such as colour, shininess, texture, and transparency.

Meissner's corpuscles Receptors for measuring touch sensations in the fingertips.

MIDI Musical Instrument Digital Interface. A standard for digital music representation.

MIME Multi-purpose Internet Mail Extension. Used to specify file-typing rules for Internet applications including browsers.

Model A geometric representation of an object produced by a CAD system or 3D modelling package.

Model board A scale model of an airport used before the introduction of VEs.

Modelling The action of building a VE.

Momentum The product of mass and velocity.

Monochrome The use of one colour as in black and white photography.

Monocular Using one eye.

Monocular depth cues Mechanisms such as motion parallax for estimating depth with one eye.

Motion parallax A monocular visual cue for estimating the depth of moving objects.

Motion platform A moving platform associated with simulators.

Motion sickness Unpleasant symptoms experienced when the brain receives conflicting visual and motion cues.

Mouse A pointing device used for controlling a screen's cursor.

MPEG Moving Picture Experts Group.

Multimedia An integrated computer presentation including graphics, audio, text, and video.

Network A set of interconnected computers.

Node The basic component of a scene graph.

NTSC National Television Standards Committee is a television standard widely used in the USA.

Object constancy   The way objects in the real world appear stationary when we move our heads.

Object picking   The action of selecting an object in a VE.

Object space   The coordinate system in which an object is defined.

Optic nerve   Connects the eye to the brain.

Orthogonal   At right angles to some datum.

Ossicular system   A system of small bones in the inner ear.

Pacinian corpuscles   Touch receptors used for detecting vibrations.

PAL   Acronym for Phase Alternation Line. A television standard used in the UK and other countries.

Palette   A collection of colours.

Paradigm   A pattern or model.

Parallax   The apparent movement of an object arising from a change in the position of the observer.

Particle system   A collection of discrete particles used to model natural phenomena.

Percentile   One of 99 actual or notional values of a variable dividing its distribution into 100 groups with equal frequencies.

Peripheral vision   Visual information detected at the periphery of our field of view (FOV).

Persistence of vision   The eye's ability to record a visual signal after the stimulus has been removed.

Perspective depth cues   Size cues that enable us to estimate depth.

Phong shading   A shading technique that introduces reflective highlights into a surface.

Photopic vision   Vision with the use of cone receptors.

Photopsin   A protein used in cone receptors.

Photo-realism   Highly realistic computer-generated scenes.

Photo-receptors   The rods and cones that convert light into nerve signals.

Physical simulation   Algorithms for simulating physical behaviour.

Picking   See **Object picking**.

Picture plane   A projection plane used to capture an image, especially for perspective projections.

Pinna   The outer part of the ear.

Pitch   The rotational angle about a horizontal X-axis, orthogonal to the forward-facing Z-axis.

Pixel   The smallest addressable picture element on a display.

Planar polygon   Has its vertices in one plane.

PNG   Portable network graphics. A specification for representing 2D images in files.

Point-and-fly   A command to initiate a flying direction and action.

Pointing device   A hardware device connected to the user's computer by which the user directly controls the location and direction of the pointer.

Polygon   A shape bounded by straight edges.

Polygonal mesh   A boundary structure formed from a collection polygons.

Polyhedron   An object having a polygonal boundary.

Polyline   A chain of straight line segments.

Portal   A virtual 'doorway' into another VE.

Presence   The sense of realism created by being immersed in a VE.

Properties   The attributes associated with an object such as colour, position, and behaviour.

Proprioceptive sensations   Monitor the status of the body, such as position, equilibrium, and muscles.

Radiosity   A global illumination model for computing light intensities resulting from multiple diffuse reflections.

RAM   An acronym for random access memory.

Raster   One line of a frame or field.

Ray tracing   Uses the geometry of light rays to render a scene.

Real time   An instantaneous reaction to any changes in signals being processed.

Refresh rate   The frequency a raster display refreshes its screen.

Renderer

(*a*) *Image*: A program for creating a shaded 3D image.

(*b*) *Acoustic*: A program for simulating sound patterns in a VE.

Rendering   The process of projecting a 3D object onto a 2D display, clipping it to fit the view, removing hidden surfaces, and shading the visible ones according to the light sources.

Resolution   A measure of a system's ability to record fine detail.

RGB   Red, green, and blue. A colour space where a colour is represented as a combin- ation of the primary colours RGB.

Rhodopsin   Light-sensitive pigment found in rod receptors.

Rigid body   An object whose geometry is fixed.

Rods   Light receptors in the retina that are active in dim lighting conditions.

Roll angle   The angle of rotation about the forward-facing heading vector.

Ruffini's end organs   Touch receptors in deep tissue that do not adapt to any extent.

Saturation   The purity of a colour in terms of the white light component and the colour component.

Scaling matrix   Changes the size of an object.

Scanner   An input device for converting photographs into a digital form.

Scene graph   An ordered collection of nodes as used in VRML.

Scotopic vision   Rod or night vision.

Scotopsin   A protein found in rhodopsin that aids the conversion of light into electricity.

Scripting language   A computer language that is interpreted and executed sequentially.

Semicircular canals   The anterior, posterior, and horizontal ducts in the vestibular system for predicting loss of equilibrium.

Shading   The process of colouring an object.

Soft objects   Objects modelled from mathematical equations.

Somatic senses   The senses of touch, pain, position, and temperature.

Spaceball   A 6 DOF pointing device manufactured by Spaceball Technologies, Inc.

Spatialized sound   Sound filtered so that it seems to be localized in 3D space.

Stereocilla   Small hairs in the vestibular system for monitoring head position.

Stereogram   An image that contains parallax information, such as random dot stereograms.

Stereopsis   The action of obtaining two views of an object with two eyes.

Stereoscope   A device for creating a stereoscopic image from a pair of images containing parallax information.

Stereoscopic   Requires two images with parallax information, giving the illusion of depth and relief.

Surface attributes   Qualities such as colour and texture.

Surface of revolution   See **Swept surface**.

Surface patch   A surface description that can be used to form a complex surface.

Surge   The forward movement of a motion platform.

Sway   The horizontal movement of a motion platform.

Swept surface   A 3D surface formed by rotating a contour about an axis.

Tactile feedback   Sensory information detected through the sense of touch.

Tactile receptors   Measure sensations of touch.

TCP/IP   Transport control protocol/Internet protocol is a networking protocol used for communications between computers. TCP provides the transport layer of the ISO OSI (open systems interconnect) model. IP provides the network layer.

Teleporting   The action of moving from one position in a VE to another.

Telepresence   Relaying a view of a scene back to some distant viewer.

Texture map   A 2D pattern image for use as surface decoration.

Texture mapping   Substituting detail stored within a texture map onto a surface.

Toolkit   A software system for building, visualizing, and interacting with VEs.

Torque   A rotational force.

Tracking   Monitoring an object's 3D position and orientation.

Triangulation   Reducing a shape into a triangular mesh.

Update rate   The rate at which a process is modified.

URL   Uniform resource locator.

Value   Is equivalent to the term lightness.

VE   See **Virtual environment**.

Vertex   The end of an edge.

Vestibular system   Monitors the acceleration, equilibrium, and relationship of body with the Earth's gravitational field.

Virtual domain   The imaginary space inside a computer.

Virtual environment (VE)   A 3D data set describing an environment based upon real-world or abstract objects and data.

Virtual hand   A simple model of a hand built into the VE.

Virtual reality (VR)   A generic term for systems that create a real-time visual/audio/haptic experience.

Virtual world   See **World**.

Visceral sensations   Record discomfort or pain from the viscera organs in the chest cavity.

Visual acuity   The ability of eye to discern fine detail.

Visual cortex   Part of the brain used for processing visual information.

Visual cues   Signals or prompts derived from a scene.

Vomit centre   Part of the brain responsible for initiating vomiting.

VR   An acronym for virtual reality.

VRML   Virtual reality modelling language.

VRML browser   See **Browser**.

VRML file   A set of VRML nodes and statements as defined in ISO/IEC 14772.

Wand   A pointing device that moves in 3D and that enables a user to indicate apo-sition in the 3D coordinate system.

Widgets   GUI controls such as menus and dialogue boxes.

Wire frame   A 3D object where all edges are drawn, producing a 'see-through' wire-like image.

World   A collection of one or more VRML files and other multimedia content that, when interpreted by a VRML browser, presents an interactive experience to the user.

World coordinate space   The Cartesian coordinate system used for locating 3D worlds.

World Wide Web   The collection of documents, data and content typically encoded in HTML pages and accessible via the Internet using the HTTP protocol.

Yaw angle   A angle of rotation about a vertical axis.

Appendix A
VRML Web Sites

The following are useful web sites for information on virtual reality modelling language (VRML):

http://193.49.43.3/dif/3D_crystals.html
http://amber.rc.arizona.edu/
http://vrml.sgi.com/cafe/
http://www.3dweb.com/
http://www.aereal.com/instant/
http://www.austin.ibm.com/vrml/
http://www.aw.sgi.com/
http://www.cgrg.ohio-state.edu/
http://www.cosmosoftware.com/
http://www.emptiness.org/vr/vr-resources.html
http://www.cybertown.com/
http://www.hash.com/
http://www.immersive.com/
http://www.itl.nist.gov/div894/ovrt/OVRThome.html
http://www.landform.com/landform.htm
http://www.macromedia.com/
http://www.micrografx.com/simply3d/
http://www.mindworkshop.com/alchemy/alchemy.html
http://www.mpic-tueb.mpg.de/projects/-vrtueb/vrtueb.html
http://www.multigen.com/
http://www.neuro.sfc.keio.ac.jp/~aly/polygon/vrml/ika/
http://www.ocnus.com/models
http://www.paradigmsim.com/
http://www.photomodeler.com/

http://www.realimation.com/
http://www.sense8.com/
http://www.sgi.com/
http://www.virtus.com/index.html
http://www.vrmlsite.com/
http://www.worlds.net/

Appendix B
HMDs

The following table identifies some head-mounted displays (HMDs) currently available:

Name	Resolution (h × v)	Overlap	Field of view
Cyber Eye	230 × 420		22.5°h × 16.8°v
Cyberface 2	319 × 117	60.6°	140°h
Cyberface 3	720 × 240	N/A	80°h
Eyegen 3	493 × 250	Variable	40° at 100% overlap
Flight Helmet	240 × 120	79%	90–100°h
HRX	416 × 277	65°	106°h × 75°v
MRG 2	240 × 240	N/A	84°h × 65°v
NASA Ames CRT	400 lines	90°	120°h per eye
NASA Ames View	640 × 220	90°	120°h
Kaiser ProView XL40STm		100%/25°	36°h × 27°v
Kaiser ProView XL50STm		100%	48°h × 27°v
Kaiser ProView XL35		100%	20°h × 21°v
Kaiser ProView XL50		100%	40°h × 30°v
Kaiser Sim Eye 100A		30°	100°h × 50°v
Quaterwave	1280 × 1024		50°h
WFOV	1280 × 1024	40°	80–110°h × 60°v
HMSI 1000	450 × 220	100%	65°h × 46°v
VIM 1000pv	800 × 225	67%, 100%	100°h × 30°v
Datavisor 80	1280 × 1024	50%	80° per eye
Stereo Viewer-1	1280 × 960	100%	57° circular

Appendix C
Trackers

The following table identifies some trackers currently available:

Product	Tech.	Positional Accuracy	Positional Resolution	Angular Accuracy	Angular Resolution
ADL-1	M	0.2 in.	0.025 in.		
BOOM	M	0.16 in.			0.1°
Logitech	A	0.004 in.	0.004 in.	0.1°	0.1°
Digisonic	A		<0.005 in.		0.1°
Ascension	E	0.1°	0.03 in.	0.5°	0.1° at 12 in.
Polhemus Isotrak II	E	0.1 in. at <30 in.	0.0015 in.	0.75° at <30 in.	0.1°
Polhemus Fastrak	E	0.03 in. at <30 in.	0.002 in.	0.15° at <30 in.	0.05°
UNC	O		<2 mm		<2°
ELITE	O	1/24,000 of field of view	1/65,536 of field of view		
Wayfinder-VR	I			±2°	±1°
Vector 2X	I			2°	2°
TCM2	I			±0.5° to ±1.5°	0.1°

Technology key: E, electromagnetic; I, inertial; M, mechanical; O, optical; A, acoustic.

Appendix D
VRML Program

This VRML 1.0 program listing is part of the VRML document located at: http:// www.vrml.org/VRML1.0/vrml10c.html.

```
#VRML V1.0 test
Separator {
  Separator {      # Simple track-light geometry:
    Translation { translation 0 4 0 }
    Separator {
      Material { emissiveColor 0.1 0.3 0.3 }
      Cube {
        width 0.1
        height 0.1
        depth 4
      }
    }
    Rotation { rotation 0 1 0 1.57079 }
    Separator {
      Material { emissiveColor 0.3 0.1 0.3 }
      Cylinder {
        radius 0.1
        height .2
      }
    }
    Rotation { rotation -1 0 0 1.57079 }
    Separator {
      Material { emissiveColor 0.3 0.3 0.1 }
      Rotation { rotation 1 0 0 1.57079 }
```

```
      Translation { translation 0 -.2 0 }
      Cone {
         height .4
         bottomRadius .2
      }
      Translation { translation 0 .4 0 }
      Cylinder {
         radius 0.02
         height .4
         }
      }
   }
   SpotLight { # Light from above
      location 0 4 0
      direction 0 -1 0
      intensity      0.9
      cutOffAngle      0.7
   }
   Separator { # Wall geometry; just three flat polygons
      Coordinate3 {
         point [
            -2 0 -2, -2 0 2, 2 0 2, 2 0 -2,
            -2 4 -2, -2 4 2, 2 4 2, 2 4 -2]
      }
      IndexedFaceSet {
         coordIndex [ 0, 1, 2, 3, -1,
               0, 4, 5, 1, -1,
               0, 3, 7, 4, -1
               ]
      }
   }
   WWWAnchor { # A hyper-linked cow:
      name "http://www.foo.edu/CowProject/AboutCows.html"
      Separator {
         Translation { translation 0 1 0 }
         WWWInline { # Reference another object
            name "http://www.foo.edu/3DObjects/cow.wrl"
         }
      }
   }
}
```

Appendix E
Web Sites for VR Products

The following sites are worth visiting to obtain more information about VR hardware and software products:

Advanced Rendering Technology	www.artvps.com
Antycip	www.antycip.com
Aveva	www.aveva.com
Blueberry3D	www.blueberry3d.com
Boston Dynamics	www.bdi.com
Deespona	www.deespona.com
Division	www.division.com
Dreamality Technologies	www.dreamalitytechnologies.com
Elumens	www.elumens.com
Essential Reality	www.essentialreality.com
Evans & Sutherland	www.es.com
Fakespace	www.fakespace.com
HITLab Washington University	www.hitl.washington.edu
Hypervision	www.hypervision.co.uk
Immersion Corporation	www.immersion.com
James Hans	www.infinite-detail.com
Lake DSP Pty.	www.lakedsp.com
Motion Analysis Corporation	www.motionanalysis.com
nVidia	www.nvidia.com
Parametric Technologies	www.ptc.com
Polhemus	www.polhemus.com
Pyramid Systems	www.pyramidsystems.com
RealityWave	www.realitywave.com
Sense8	www.sense8.com

Silicon Graphics	www.sgi.com
Spacetec IM	www.spacetec.com
Stereographics	www.stereographics.com
Transom Corporation	www.transom.com
Trimension	www.trimension-inc.com
Viewpoint DataLabs	www.viewpoint.com
Virtual Presence	www.vrweb.com
Virtual Research	www.virtualresearch.com
VR Centre, Teesside University	www.vr-centre.com

References

Blinn, J.F. (1978) Simulation of wrinkled surfaces. *SIGGRAPH* **78**, 286–292.

Blinn, J.F. and Newell, M.E. (1976) Texture and reflection in computer generated images. *Comm. ACM* **19**, 542–547.

Gouraud, H. (1971) *Computer Display of Curved Surfaces.* Ph.D. Thesis, University of Utah.

Guyton, A.C. (1991) *Textbook of Medical Physiology.* Philadelphia: W.B. Saunders Company.

Hartman, J. and Wernecke, J. (1996) *The VRML 2.0 Handbook: Building Moving Worlds on the Web.* Addison-Wesley.

Hollands, R. (1995) Sourceless trackers. *VR News* **4(3)**, 23–29.

Julesz, B. (1971) *Foundations of Cyclopean Perception.* University of Chicago Press.

Kamat, V.V. (1993) A survey of techniques for simulation of dynamic collision detection and response. *Comput. Graph.* **17(4)**, 379–385.

Peitgen, H. and Saupe, D. (Eds) (1988) *The Science of Fractal Images.* New York: Springer-Verlag.

Phong, B. (1973) *Illumination for Computer Generated Images.* Ph.D. Thesis, University of Utah; also in *Comm. ACM* **18**, 311–317.

Plenge, G. (1974) On the difference between localization and lateralization. *J. Acoust. Soc. Am.* **56**, 944–951.

Shaw, E.A.G. (1974) The external ear. In: Keidel, W.D. and Neff, W.D., Eds *Handbook of Sensory Physiology.* New York: Springer-Verlag.

Sutherland, I.E. (1965) The ultimate display. *Proc. IFIP Cong.* **2**, 506–508.

Tidwell, M., Johnston, R.S., Melville, D. and Furness III, T.A. (1995) The virtual retinal display – a retinal scanning imaging system. *Proc. VR World*, 325–334.

Vince, J.A. (1995) *Virtual Reality Systems.* Wokingham: Addison-Wesley.

Williams, L. (1983) Pyramidal parametrics. *SIGGRAPH* **83**, 1–11.

Index